MAPI: Business Communications Integration

James Relington

DEDICATION

To those who seek knowledge, inspiration, and new perspectives—
may this book be a companion on your journey, a spark for curiosity,
and a reminder that every page turned is a step toward discovery.

AKNOWLEDGEMENTS

I would like to express my deepest gratitude to everyone who contributed to the creation of this book. To my colleagues and mentors, your insights and expertise have been invaluable. A special thank you to my family and friends for their unwavering support and encouragement throughout this journey.

The Rise of Business Communication Technologies

The way businesses communicate has always been a critical factor in their ability to operate, expand, and compete in evolving markets. From the earliest days of handwritten letters and telegrams to today's instant messaging and integrated digital platforms, communication technologies have shaped every aspect of business strategy and execution. Over the last century, few areas have experienced as much transformation as the tools and systems organizations use to share information both internally and externally.

In the early 20th century, business communication was heavily reliant on paper-based correspondence, physical memos, and face-to-face meetings. The speed at which information traveled was limited by geography and logistics. International communication, for example, could take weeks to complete a single transaction or negotiation, often leading to delays and inefficiencies. Businesses invested heavily in postal services and telegraphy to overcome some of these limitations, but these solutions were still constrained by the physical infrastructure available at the time.

The introduction of the telephone marked a revolutionary shift. For the first time, businesses could engage in real-time, voice-to-voice conversations across great distances. The telephone shortened decision-making cycles and facilitated quicker customer service, supplier coordination, and management oversight. This new immediacy provided a competitive edge to companies that could afford and effectively implement telephone systems in their operations. However, voice communication was just one piece of the puzzle. As organizations grew in complexity and size, the need for systematic, recordable, and traceable communication methods became increasingly apparent.

By the mid-20th century, fax machines and early computing devices began to make their way into corporate environments. Fax technology allowed documents to be sent over telephone lines, reducing the time it took to share contracts, proposals, and reports. Around the same period, large enterprises began experimenting with mainframe computers to store and process business data. While these early systems were primitive compared to modern standards, they laid the groundwork for digitized information exchange.

The arrival of personal computers in the 1980s was a catalyst for even greater change. With the widespread adoption of PCs and local area networks (LANs), businesses could now create internal networks that facilitated email communication, file sharing, and data collaboration among employees. Email emerged as the dominant tool for business communication, offering speed, documentation, and flexibility. The corporate world quickly realized the value of asynchronous communication, which allowed employees to send and receive messages without the need for both parties to be present simultaneously, as was the case with phone calls.

As the internet expanded in the 1990s, business communication entered a new era. The global reach of the internet removed geographic barriers and gave rise to new models of collaboration, such as virtual teams and international partnerships. Organizations could now access information, engage with clients, and manage operations on a global scale. Video conferencing, made possible by increasing bandwidth and more sophisticated software, introduced a new dynamic to business meetings. Companies no longer needed to rely solely on costly business trips to conduct negotiations or manage teams abroad.

Simultaneously, the development of enterprise resource planning (ERP) systems and customer relationship management (CRM) tools integrated communication functions with core business processes. These platforms allowed businesses to streamline operations, enhance customer engagement, and make data-driven decisions. Information was no longer isolated in departmental silos; instead, it could flow seamlessly across various functions, improving overall efficiency and responsiveness.

The early 2000s witnessed the explosive growth of mobile technology, further transforming business communication. Smartphones and tablets allowed employees to remain connected while traveling or working remotely. This mobility blurred the boundaries between work and personal life, enabling real-time decision-making and collaboration from virtually anywhere. Applications such as mobile email, instant messaging, and project management tools became essential components of the modern business toolkit.

Today, cloud computing, artificial intelligence, and integrated communication platforms are redefining the landscape once again. Tools such as Slack, Microsoft Teams, and Zoom offer unified communication environments where chat, video, file sharing, and workflow automation coexist. Businesses now expect their communication systems to do more than simply transmit information; they demand platforms that integrate with existing business applications, provide analytics, and enhance team productivity through automation and intelligent recommendations.

The shift towards remote work and distributed teams, accelerated by global events such as the COVID-19 pandemic, has cemented the role of digital communication technologies in the corporate world. Organizations of all sizes have had to rapidly adopt or upgrade their communication infrastructure to ensure business continuity and employee engagement. Asynchronous and synchronous tools are now working in tandem to accommodate the diverse needs of global teams operating across different time zones and cultural contexts.

Business communication technologies continue to evolve at a rapid pace, driven by advances in cloud computing, machine learning, and cybersecurity. The integration of AI into communication platforms is leading to smarter email filtering, real-time language translation, automated meeting summaries, and sentiment analysis in customer interactions. Moreover, businesses are increasingly focused on protecting their communications with advanced encryption protocols and compliance mechanisms to meet the growing demands of data privacy regulations worldwide.

The rise of business communication technologies reflects a larger trend toward greater agility, scalability, and interconnectedness in the business ecosystem. What once required days or weeks can now be accomplished in seconds, and organizations that master these tools gain a substantial competitive advantage. The integration of communication technologies into everyday business operations has become not just a facilitator but a critical driver of success in the digital economy.

MAPI: An Introduction to Messaging Application Programming Interface

Messaging Application Programming Interface, widely known as MAPI, is a powerful and foundational technology that has significantly influenced how organizations manage and streamline communication processes within enterprise environments. Initially developed by Microsoft in the early 1990s, MAPI was designed as a comprehensive interface that enables client applications to communicate with messaging servers, particularly Microsoft Exchange Server. The objective behind the creation of MAPI was to provide a standardized set of tools for developers and businesses to build robust email and messaging solutions, allowing seamless interaction with messaging systems.

At its core, MAPI serves as an API that bridges applications with email systems, offering access to messaging functions such as sending and receiving emails, managing calendars, handling contacts, and even controlling tasks and notes. Unlike simple email protocols such as SMTP, POP3, or IMAP, MAPI provides a much deeper and more integrated connection to messaging infrastructure. It goes beyond the basic transmission of messages by giving applications the ability to interact with message stores, address books, and messaging transport services in a highly controlled and feature-rich manner.

MAPI is divided into two primary categories: Simple MAPI and Extended MAPI. Simple MAPI provides basic messaging functions, including the ability to send and receive emails and access address books. This version was designed for simpler applications where full control of the messaging system was not necessary. On the other hand, Extended MAPI offers a complete set of features that allow developers to manipulate the messaging environment at a granular level. With Extended MAPI, applications can create custom message stores, manage user profiles, manipulate folders and messages, and even interact directly with the messaging transport providers.

One of the key strengths of MAPI is its ability to integrate deeply with Microsoft Exchange Server. This integration enables client applications such as Microsoft Outlook to leverage the full range of collaboration and messaging capabilities offered by Exchange. Through MAPI, Outlook clients can perform actions such as scheduling meetings, booking conference rooms, setting delegate access permissions, and managing public folders—all from a single unified interface. This level of integration has been a cornerstone in driving the adoption of Exchange Server and Outlook in enterprises around the world, solidifying MAPI's relevance in corporate communication infrastructures.

MAPI operates on a client-server model where the client, such as an email application, interacts with the server through MAPI calls. These calls are processed by service providers, which handle various aspects of the messaging ecosystem. Service providers in the MAPI architecture include the Message Store Provider, which manages access to the message database; the Address Book Provider, which offers access to contact directories; and the Transport Provider, which handles the actual delivery and receipt of messages. Each of these providers works together to deliver a seamless messaging experience to the end user and the applications involved.

In addition to its native support for Microsoft environments, MAPI has also been utilized in custom enterprise applications that require integrated messaging functionality. Many organizations have leveraged MAPI to build applications that automate business processes, such as generating reports that are automatically emailed to designated recipients or creating workflow systems that send notifications and alerts based on specific triggers. MAPI's flexibility has allowed businesses to tailor their messaging workflows to meet unique operational needs.

Security is another aspect where MAPI plays a crucial role. As business communications contain sensitive and confidential information, MAPI includes mechanisms for message encryption and secure transport. When used with Microsoft Exchange and Outlook, MAPI supports various security protocols, including SSL/TLS and S/MIME, to ensure the confidentiality, integrity, and authenticity of messages. Furthermore, MAPI's integration with enterprise-level authentication systems, such as Active Directory, enhances security by enabling single sign-on (SSO) and role-based access control.

Over the years, MAPI has continued to evolve to meet the demands of modern business environments. One of its major advancements came with the introduction of MAPI over HTTP, a protocol that replaces the older RPC (Remote Procedure Call) over HTTP mechanism. MAPI over HTTP is designed to be more efficient, reliable, and resilient, particularly in remote and cloud-based scenarios. It improves user experience by providing faster reconnection times, better error handling, and enhanced support for contemporary networking environments, including mobile and remote access.

Despite the rise of RESTful APIs and cloud-native communication protocols, MAPI remains a critical component in many enterprises, especially those with significant investments in Microsoft Exchange and Outlook ecosystems. While modern developers might gravitate toward REST-based solutions, particularly with the increasing adoption of Microsoft Graph API, MAPI's deep-rooted presence in legacy systems and its rich feature set ensure that it continues to be a relevant and valuable tool for integrating messaging capabilities into business applications.

MAPI's influence extends beyond just email. Through its comprehensive API set, it also supports calendar synchronization, task management, and contact management, helping businesses create cohesive and interconnected platforms that foster productivity and collaboration. By enabling direct interaction with the data structures of Exchange and Outlook, MAPI facilitates the creation of custom solutions that align with an organization's workflow and business objectives.

As businesses continue to navigate digital transformation, MAPI stands as a testament to the enduring importance of adaptable and robust communication technologies. The ability to bridge applications and messaging systems efficiently has empowered companies to streamline operations, reduce manual tasks, and create more responsive and dynamic communication networks. For IT administrators and developers alike, understanding MAPI opens the door to crafting solutions that not only enhance messaging capabilities but also align tightly with enterprise systems and processes.

The Foundations of Business Communications Integration

Business communications integration has become one of the most vital pillars for modern organizations aiming to operate effectively and competitively in a connected world. The ability to unify various communication channels, data flows, and business applications into a seamless ecosystem is no longer a luxury but a necessity for operational excellence. Understanding the foundations of business communications integration is key to comprehending how organizations harness technology to break down silos, improve workflows, and drive collaborative success across all levels of the enterprise.

At its essence, business communications integration is the process of connecting disparate communication systems—such as email, instant messaging, voice, video conferencing, and collaboration platforms—into a unified architecture that supports both internal operations and external interactions with clients, partners, and vendors. Historically, communication tools in businesses operated in isolation. Email servers handled electronic correspondence, phone systems operated independently, and face-to-face meetings were the standard for collaboration. This fragmented approach limited the ability to respond quickly to dynamic business environments and led to inefficiencies in how information flowed across departments and teams.

The technological shift that started in the late 20th century, driven by networking advancements and the rise of enterprise software solutions, paved the way for the integration of communication platforms. The goal was to create an interconnected environment where employees could access information and communicate across multiple channels without switching between separate systems or manually transferring data. Early forms of integration focused on linking email systems to customer relationship management software or connecting telephony with service desks. These initial steps revealed the productivity gains that could be achieved by reducing redundancies and automating routine communication processes.

A fundamental component of business communications integration is interoperability. Interoperability refers to the ability of different software systems, applications, and devices to exchange data and function cohesively. To achieve this, businesses began adopting APIs (Application Programming Interfaces), middleware, and standardized communication protocols. APIs became instrumental in enabling applications to interact and share data in real time, while middleware provided the necessary bridges to connect legacy systems with newer platforms. Standard protocols like SMTP, IMAP, SIP, and MAPI served as the backbone that allowed for consistent data exchange and message transmission across diverse platforms.

Equally important in the foundations of integration is the concept of workflow optimization. Effective communication is more than the transmission of information; it is about how that information supports processes and decision-making. Integration allows businesses to automate critical workflows. For example, when a customer service agent receives an escalation email, the system can automatically trigger a notification in a project management tool, log a case in the CRM, and schedule a follow-up call—all without manual input. This level of automation minimizes human error, ensures timely responses, and streamlines operations, giving businesses a distinct advantage in responsiveness and efficiency.

Another crucial aspect is data centralization. In traditional, non-integrated communication environments, valuable information becomes scattered across multiple systems, making it difficult for decision-makers to access a comprehensive view of operations. Business communications integration consolidates data into unified repositories where emails, chat logs, call records, and meeting notes can be cross-referenced and analyzed in context. This centralized approach supports better analytics, trend identification, and strategic planning. Moreover, it ensures that teams are working with consistent and up-to-date information, reducing the risks of miscommunication and duplicated efforts.

Security and compliance also form an integral part of the foundational framework of business communications integration. Modern enterprises are subject to stringent regulations governing how they handle sensitive data, including communications. Integration frameworks must be designed with security in mind, ensuring encrypted data exchanges, secure user authentication, and access control mechanisms. Furthermore, integrated systems enable businesses to enforce consistent compliance policies across all communication channels. For instance, email archiving, call recording, and data retention policies can be uniformly applied to meet regulatory requirements, regardless of the channel used to transmit or store the information.

Scalability is another foundational principle that shapes how businesses approach communication integration. As organizations grow, so does the complexity of their operations and the volume of their communications. A well-designed integration framework must be able to accommodate the increasing demands of a larger workforce, multiple locations, and a growing ecosystem of third-party applications. Cloud-based platforms and microservices architectures have become essential in supporting scalable communication integrations, enabling businesses to expand or adapt their systems without major overhauls.

Collaboration is at the heart of integrated communications. By breaking down barriers between teams and enabling cross-functional interaction through unified platforms, businesses can cultivate a culture of shared knowledge and innovation. Integrated communications enable real-time collaboration, allowing geographically dispersed teams to work together as if they were in the same physical location. Tools such as instant messaging, video conferencing, and file sharing are no longer isolated utilities but interconnected elements of a broader, more cohesive communication strategy.

The evolution of business communications integration has also been shaped by the rise of customer-centricity in modern enterprises. Businesses now recognize that efficient internal communication directly influences customer experience. Integrated communication systems allow sales, support, marketing, and operations teams to work in concert, providing clients with faster responses, more accurate information, and personalized service. The seamless sharing of data and communication histories ensures that all stakeholders have the context they need to deliver high-quality service.

The role of integration platforms such as Microsoft Exchange, MAPI, unified communication systems, and API gateways has been pivotal in this journey. These tools provide the technical foundation that supports the seamless interaction of diverse applications and communication channels. Through continuous advancements, businesses are now able to leverage artificial intelligence, machine learning, and advanced analytics within their communication ecosystems, further optimizing workflows and enabling predictive decision-making.

The foundations of business communications integration are rooted in the need for agility, efficiency, and alignment within an increasingly complex digital landscape. As organizations continue to embrace hybrid work models, global operations, and rapid technological change, integrated communication systems are essential to sustaining collaboration and maintaining a competitive edge. Whether through email, voice, video, or real-time chat, the ability to unify communication into a synchronized and intelligent framework remains one of the most transformative drivers of business success.

The Evolution of Email Systems and MAPI

The history of email systems is a story of continuous technological advancement, driven by the need for faster, more reliable, and more efficient communication within and between organizations. What began as a simple method for sending electronic messages between two users on the same network has evolved into a complex infrastructure that supports global business operations. At the center of this evolution stands MAPI, the Messaging Application Programming Interface, which has played a crucial role in shaping modern email systems, particularly within enterprise environments.

The earliest email systems in the 1960s and 1970s were limited to academic and government institutions. These rudimentary systems operated on closed networks, allowing users to send basic text messages from one terminal to another. These messages were stored in specific directories on mainframe computers, and there were no standardized protocols to govern the process. Communication was largely asynchronous, with users accessing their messages when they logged into the same system. This was far removed from the highly integrated email ecosystems of today, but it laid the initial groundwork for electronic messaging.

As organizations grew and networking technology advanced, the need for email systems that could operate across different networks became apparent. The development of protocols such as SMTP (Simple Mail Transfer Protocol) and later POP3 (Post Office Protocol) and IMAP (Internet Message Access Protocol) in the 1980s and early 1990s allowed email systems to move beyond isolated environments. SMTP enabled the sending of messages between servers, while POP3 and IMAP provided mechanisms for retrieving and managing messages on client devices. These protocols brought greater flexibility and accessibility to email, making it a practical tool for businesses seeking faster internal and external communication.

The emergence of graphical user interfaces and personal computers further accelerated the adoption of email. Applications like Microsoft Mail, Lotus Notes, and Eudora introduced user-friendly interfaces that made email accessible to a broader audience within companies. These early email clients were mostly standalone systems, handling email independently of other business applications. However, as companies began to rely more heavily on email for day-to-day operations, the limitations of these basic systems became evident. Email needed to be more than a simple messaging service; it needed to integrate with other essential business tools.

It was during this phase that MAPI emerged as a key enabler of deeper integration between email clients and enterprise messaging servers. Introduced by Microsoft in the early 1990s, MAPI was designed to allow applications to interact directly with messaging servers like Microsoft Exchange. Unlike SMTP, POP3, or IMAP, which primarily handled message transport and retrieval, MAPI provided a complete framework for interacting with the entire messaging system. This included access to not only messages but also calendars, contacts, tasks, and public folders.

MAPI fundamentally changed how businesses could use email. By allowing applications such as Microsoft Outlook to integrate seamlessly with Exchange Server, MAPI enabled users to manage emails, schedule meetings, access shared address books, and collaborate on projects from a single interface. It supported both synchronous and asynchronous operations and offered robust security and administrative features. The introduction of Extended MAPI gave developers the ability to create custom solutions tailored to specific business needs, making MAPI an indispensable component of enterprise IT strategies.

Over the years, Microsoft Exchange Server evolved alongside MAPI. Early versions of Exchange offered basic email and directory services, but later iterations incorporated enhanced collaboration tools, improved security, and better scalability. MAPI played a critical role in this evolution, acting as the communication bridge between the Exchange server and client applications. It allowed for more dynamic communication workflows, where information could flow effortlessly between emails, meeting invitations, task assignments, and contact records.

MAPI also enabled new levels of automation in email workflows. Businesses could now build applications that leveraged MAPI to automatically send reports, generate notifications, or synchronize data between the messaging system and other enterprise applications like CRM platforms or ERP systems. The ability to integrate messaging functionality into custom business processes was a game-changer for organizations seeking to improve efficiency and reduce manual work.

The evolution of email systems continued with the growth of the internet and the shift towards cloud computing. As organizations began to adopt cloud-based services, Microsoft adapted MAPI to function in new environments. One significant milestone was the development of MAPI over HTTP, which replaced the older RPC over HTTP transport. This new protocol improved connection stability, reduced latency, and enhanced compatibility with modern network infrastructures. MAPI over HTTP also offered better resilience for remote and mobile workers, reflecting the growing importance of flexible work environments.

At the same time, competing standards and APIs emerged, such as REST-based services and Microsoft Graph API. While these newer technologies provide lightweight, web-friendly alternatives to MAPI for integrating cloud-based Microsoft 365 services, MAPI retains a crucial role in many organizations, particularly those with on-premises Exchange environments or hybrid deployments. MAPI's rich feature set and deep integration capabilities ensure that it continues to be used for advanced email system functions that require direct access to messaging data stores and server-side components.

The role of email has expanded beyond simple text-based communication. Today's email systems, powered in part by MAPI, support multimedia attachments, encryption, digital signatures, collaborative editing, and integration with project management and customer service platforms. Enterprise email is now part of a larger ecosystem of unified communication tools, where chat, video conferencing, and document sharing coexist within a cohesive digital workplace.

MAPI's legacy and continued relevance lie in its ability to adapt to changing technological landscapes. From the early days of simple message delivery to the modern, integrated business communication platforms of today, MAPI has been a foundational technology driving the evolution of enterprise email systems. It has enabled businesses to create richer, more connected experiences for their users, bringing email out of isolation and embedding it into the broader context of organizational workflows and decision-making processes.

MAPI Architecture: A Technical Overview

The Messaging Application Programming Interface, commonly referred to as MAPI, is a complex and highly structured framework that enables robust communication between client applications and messaging servers. Designed by Microsoft, MAPI provides developers and systems integrators with a powerful toolkit for building applications that interact directly with email servers, particularly Microsoft Exchange. To fully understand the capabilities and operational flexibility of MAPI, it is essential to explore its architecture, which is composed of a series of interdependent layers and components working together to provide seamless messaging functionality.

At the core of MAPI architecture lies its client-server model, where the client application, such as Microsoft Outlook or any MAPI-compliant program, communicates with a messaging server like Microsoft Exchange Server. The client leverages MAPI's API calls to request access to messaging services, such as sending emails, retrieving calendar appointments, or accessing address books. The server responds to these requests through a series of service providers, which abstract the complexities of the messaging infrastructure and deliver the required data or functionality back to the client. This model ensures that applications can focus on business logic without needing to manage the underlying messaging system.

The MAPI subsystem, which resides on the client side, serves as the primary interface that applications use to access messaging functions. It is responsible for loading the necessary service providers and coordinating communication between them and the client application. The subsystem provides a rich set of APIs organized into different objects, including sessions, message stores, folders, messages, attachments, address books, and tables. Each object offers a series of methods and properties that allow developers to perform fine-grained operations. For example, the message object allows applications to create, modify, or delete individual messages, while the folder object manages collections of messages and subfolders within the message store.

Service providers form a critical layer in MAPI's architecture, functioning as modular components that handle specific aspects of the messaging environment. There are three main types of service providers in a typical MAPI implementation: the Message Store Provider, the Address Book Provider, and the Transport Provider. The Message Store Provider is responsible for managing access to the physical storage where email messages, folders, and other messaging items are maintained. It handles operations such as creating folders, retrieving message content, and managing metadata. The Address Book Provider offers a standardized interface for accessing and searching contact directories, enabling client applications to resolve recipient names and manage distribution lists. The Transport Provider oversees the delivery and receipt of messages between the client and the server, ensuring that messages are transmitted securely and reliably across the network.

An essential feature of MAPI's design is its extensibility. Developers can create custom service providers to integrate non-standard or proprietary systems into the MAPI framework. For instance, an organization could build a transport provider that routes messages through an alternative messaging platform or a message store provider that connects to a non-Microsoft database. This extensibility makes MAPI particularly appealing to enterprises with unique business needs or legacy systems that require specialized integration.

Another fundamental component of MAPI architecture is the session layer. A session is a logical context established between the client application and the MAPI subsystem. It acts as a container for all operations performed by the client during a single interaction with the messaging system. The session maintains authentication credentials, security tokens, and configuration settings required to access message stores and other resources. Once a session is established, it provides a consistent environment for the client to navigate through different folders, retrieve messages, and interact with other objects.

The MAPI property model is another key architectural element that differentiates it from simpler messaging protocols. Every MAPI object is characterized by a set of properties, which are name-value pairs representing various attributes of the object. For example, a message object might have properties such as subject, sender, recipients, message body, and attachments. Properties can be standard (defined by Microsoft) or custom (defined by the developer). This flexible property model allows applications to store additional metadata and business-specific information alongside standard messaging data, enabling greater customization of workflows and integrations.

MAPI also defines a robust notification system, which allows client applications to subscribe to events generated by the messaging system. Through notifications, applications can monitor changes to message stores, folders, or specific items and react to these changes in real time. For instance, an application could be notified when a new email arrives in a monitored folder, triggering an automated workflow or alert. This event-driven approach enhances the responsiveness of MAPI-enabled applications and supports dynamic business processes.

Security is deeply embedded within the MAPI architecture. Authentication and authorization are typically managed through integration with Microsoft's Active Directory, ensuring that only authorized users and applications have access to sensitive messaging data. MAPI also supports transport-level security through SSL/TLS and message-level encryption through technologies like S/MIME. These security features help organizations meet compliance requirements and protect their communications from unauthorized access and data breaches.

Over time, MAPI has evolved to support modern deployment scenarios. The introduction of MAPI over HTTP marked a significant shift in how MAPI communicates with Exchange servers. By leveraging standard HTTP protocols, MAPI over HTTP improves connection resiliency, supports modern firewall and proxy configurations, and enhances performance in remote and cloud-based environments. This evolution aligns with contemporary IT trends, such as hybrid cloud deployments and mobile workforces, ensuring that MAPI remains a viable option for organizations with diverse infrastructure needs.

MAPI's architecture is inherently complex, reflecting the broad range of functions it provides. It does not merely enable the sending and receiving of email; it facilitates comprehensive interaction with enterprise messaging environments. By combining session management, service providers, a versatile object and property model, and secure transport mechanisms, MAPI enables organizations to build highly integrated, scalable, and secure communication systems. This architecture underpins the success of widely used applications like Microsoft Outlook while also supporting countless custom business solutions tailored to specific operational requirements.

Core Components of MAPI in Business Environments

The Messaging Application Programming Interface, or MAPI, plays a critical role in the technological landscape of modern business environments. By providing a unified framework to manage messaging operations, MAPI allows organizations to seamlessly integrate email, calendaring, task management, contact directories, and various collaborative functions into their daily operations. Understanding the core components of MAPI is essential to appreciating how this architecture enables secure, scalable, and efficient communication workflows in businesses of all sizes.

At the heart of MAPI lies the concept of the session. The session is the starting point for all MAPI interactions, serving as the environment in which client applications establish communication with the messaging system. Every time a MAPI-enabled application, such as Microsoft Outlook, initiates a connection to the Exchange server, a session is created. This session handles authentication, maintains the context for all operations, and acts as the container for subsequent interactions with other MAPI components. In a business setting, this session is often integrated with enterprise authentication services like Microsoft Active Directory, allowing users to access messaging services securely with single sign-on capabilities.

Once a session is established, client applications rely on the message store provider to access the database where all messaging items reside. The message store is one of the foundational components of MAPI, responsible for organizing and storing emails, folders, calendars, tasks, contacts, and public folders. Each user typically has a primary message store associated with their mailbox, which is structured hierarchically to include various folders such as Inbox, Sent Items, Calendar, and custom folders created by the user. The message store allows client applications to read, write, and manipulate these messaging items. In business environments, the ability to programmatically interact with the message store allows for sophisticated automation, such as archiving old emails, generating reports based on message metadata, or automatically categorizing incoming communications.

Closely linked to the message store is the folder object, which acts as a container for messages and other items. Folders serve as organizational units that help businesses maintain structured and efficient email management practices. The Inbox folder, for instance, collects all incoming emails, while subfolders can be created to categorize messages by project, client, or department. In collaborative business environments, public folders are frequently used to share information between teams, enabling multiple users to access shared documents, contacts, or discussion threads. MAPI provides applications with the ability to create, delete, move, or modify folders as part of customized workflows tailored to business needs.

Within these folders, the message object is the core unit of communication. Each message represents an email, meeting request, task assignment, or other collaborative item. The message object encapsulates a variety of properties such as sender, recipients, subject line, message body, attachments, and timestamps. MAPI enables granular control over each of these elements. For example, businesses can use MAPI to automatically append disclaimers to outgoing emails, filter incoming messages for specific keywords, or ensure that certain attachments are removed before delivery. Beyond emails, the message object also accommodates meeting invitations and task assignments, making it a versatile element in business communication workflows.

The address book provider is another indispensable component of MAPI, giving client applications access to organizational directories. In business environments, this provider integrates with directory services like Active Directory to present a centralized, searchable database of employees, departments, distribution lists, and external contacts. Through the address book, users and applications can resolve email addresses, create mailing lists, and apply role-based access permissions. For example, when composing an email or scheduling a meeting, the address book allows users to search for recipients by name, title, or department, streamlining internal communication and collaboration. MAPI's address book provider also supports offline access, enabling users to interact with cached directory information even when disconnected from the network.

A key component responsible for message transport is the transport provider. This service ensures that messages created within the client application are delivered to the appropriate recipients, whether internal or external to the organization. In the case of Microsoft Exchange environments, the transport provider works in conjunction with Exchange transport services to route messages through the enterprise network or out to the internet. The transport provider also handles tasks such as message queuing, retrying failed deliveries, and logging delivery status. In business settings, reliability and security are paramount, and MAPI's transport provider supports encrypted transmission channels and integrates with security solutions like data loss prevention and antivirus scanning tools.

One of the strengths of MAPI is its robust property model. Every object in the MAPI hierarchy—whether a message, folder, contact, or calendar event—is defined by a series of properties. These properties represent the metadata and content of the object. For instance, a calendar event object would contain properties for start and end times, attendees, location, recurrence pattern, and notes. The extensibility of this property model allows businesses to add custom metadata to objects, which can be leveraged for workflow automation, compliance tagging, or integration with third-party applications such as CRM or project management tools. The ability to create and manage custom properties provides organizations with flexibility to tailor their communication systems to specific business processes.

MAPI also incorporates a sophisticated notification system that enables real-time updates for client applications. Whenever a change occurs in the message store—such as the arrival of a new email, modification of a contact, or creation of a calendar event—the system generates notifications that can trigger automated responses or user alerts. In business environments, this is used extensively to ensure that employees receive timely information. Applications might be configured to automatically update dashboards, send push notifications to mobile devices, or escalate urgent messages to management based on predefined rules.

Security and compliance requirements are integral to business environments, and MAPI is designed with these considerations in mind. The architecture supports integration with enterprise-level security frameworks, enforcing encryption, authentication, and access control at multiple levels. MAPI works seamlessly with security protocols such as SSL/TLS for transport encryption and S/MIME for message-level encryption and digital signatures. This ensures that sensitive communications are protected both during transmission and at rest. Compliance features such as message journaling, retention policies, and audit logging can also be enforced at the MAPI level, helping businesses meet regulatory obligations across industries.

Together, these core components of MAPI create a powerful and flexible platform that underpins the communication systems of countless businesses around the world. From managing the lifecycle of messages and organizing information hierarchically in folders to enabling directory lookups and automating workflows, MAPI provides the essential building blocks for highly integrated and efficient messaging infrastructures. Its role in connecting client applications like Outlook with enterprise servers such as Exchange ensures that business communication remains consistent, secure, and deeply embedded within broader business processes.

Setting Up a MAPI-Based Communication Framework

Implementing a MAPI-based communication framework is a strategic undertaking that empowers businesses to unify their messaging systems with other enterprise applications, creating a highly integrated and efficient communication ecosystem. MAPI, or Messaging Application Programming Interface, is specifically designed to enable client applications to interface directly with messaging servers like Microsoft Exchange. Setting up this framework involves a combination of infrastructure readiness, client configuration, security considerations, and workflow design to fully leverage the capabilities that MAPI offers.

The process begins with establishing the foundational infrastructure required to support MAPI communications. The centerpiece of any MAPI framework is the Microsoft Exchange Server, which serves as the messaging backbone for the organization. Exchange must be deployed and configured to handle mailboxes, distribution lists, calendar services, public folders, and transport services. A well-architected Exchange environment should account for scalability, redundancy, and fault tolerance to ensure reliable service delivery across the enterprise. Businesses often implement Exchange in a high-availability configuration, utilizing database availability groups (DAGs) and load balancers to minimize downtime and support mission-critical operations.

Once the Exchange environment is in place, client systems must be prepared to interact with it through MAPI. The most common MAPI-enabled client is Microsoft Outlook, which is deeply integrated with Exchange via the MAPI protocol. During the setup process, Outlook is installed on end-user devices and configured to connect to the Exchange server using the appropriate user credentials. When configured properly, Outlook establishes a MAPI session that provides full access to the user's mailbox, including email, calendar items, contacts, tasks, and notes. For large enterprises, automated deployment tools such as Group Policy or Microsoft Endpoint Configuration Manager are often used to streamline the installation and configuration of Outlook across hundreds or thousands of devices.

One of the critical aspects of setting up a MAPI-based framework is the implementation of MAPI over HTTP. This transport protocol replaces the older RPC over HTTP mechanism and is now the preferred method for connecting Outlook clients to Exchange. MAPI over HTTP provides more stable connections, better resilience in environments with high latency or intermittent connectivity, and improved support for modern network configurations including firewalls, proxies, and cloud-based deployments. To enable MAPI over HTTP, Exchange administrators must configure virtual directories on the Client Access Server (CAS) and ensure SSL certificates are properly installed to secure communications.

Beyond Outlook, other client applications may also be designed or customized to interact with the Exchange server using MAPI. Many businesses develop in-house applications that leverage Extended MAPI to automate communication workflows or integrate messaging features directly into line-of-business applications. This could include systems that automatically send reports, notifications, or alerts based on specific business events. Setting up these custom applications requires developers to utilize MAPI libraries and APIs, linking their software to the messaging infrastructure. Testing and validation are crucial to ensure that these applications comply with organizational security policies and perform reliably under real-world conditions.

Security considerations are paramount when establishing a MAPI-based communication framework. MAPI sessions typically integrate with the organization's Active Directory for user authentication and authorization, providing centralized management of user identities and access permissions. Administrators should enforce strong authentication methods, such as multi-factor authentication (MFA), to prevent unauthorized access to sensitive messaging data. Additionally, MAPI communications should be encrypted using SSL/TLS to safeguard data during transit. Configuring Exchange to support

S/MIME allows organizations to implement message-level encryption and digital signatures, adding an extra layer of protection to email communications.

Another important step is configuring and managing service providers within the MAPI framework. The three core service providers—the Message Store Provider, the Address Book Provider, and the Transport Provider—must be correctly configured to ensure seamless operation. The Message Store Provider allows client applications to access mailbox contents and public folders. The Address Book Provider connects clients to the organization's Global Address List (GAL) and offline address books, facilitating user lookups and distribution list management. The Transport Provider manages message delivery and receipt, interfacing with the Exchange transport services to ensure messages are routed correctly inside and outside the organization. Each of these providers plays a vital role in ensuring end-to-end messaging functionality and must be tuned to meet the specific needs of the business.

Beyond the technical setup, businesses must also define the workflows and policies that govern how MAPI-enabled systems will be used. This includes setting email retention policies, message size limits, attachment controls, and archiving procedures. Administrators should also define automated rules and policies for client applications to enforce consistency across the organization. For example, automated categorization of incoming messages, approval workflows triggered by calendar bookings, or flagging high-priority messages based on predefined business rules can all be implemented through MAPI's integration capabilities.

Monitoring and maintenance are essential components of a successful MAPI-based communication framework. Exchange administrators should configure logging and alerting mechanisms to detect and respond to issues related to MAPI connectivity, message delivery failures, or performance bottlenecks. Tools like Exchange Monitoring or third-party management suites can provide real-time insights into system health, user activity, and service availability. Additionally, regular reviews of the MAPI-based framework should be conducted to ensure that it continues to meet the evolving needs of the business, especially as new applications, teams, or locations are added to the environment.

With the increasing adoption of cloud services, businesses often deploy MAPI in hybrid environments, where on-premises Exchange servers coexist with cloud-based solutions like Microsoft 365. In such cases, MAPI configurations must be adapted to support hybrid functionality, allowing users to access their mailboxes whether they are hosted on-premises or in the cloud. The use of hybrid connectors, directory synchronization, and federation services ensures that the MAPI experience remains consistent across both environments.

Establishing a MAPI-based communication framework represents a significant opportunity for businesses to unify and optimize their messaging and collaboration infrastructure. By providing a reliable, secure, and highly integrated environment, MAPI helps organizations improve productivity, streamline communication processes, and enhance the user experience. When implemented thoughtfully, a MAPI framework not only meets current business requirements but also provides a scalable foundation for future growth and technological innovation.

Integrating Legacy Systems with MAPI

The integration of legacy systems with modern communication frameworks such as MAPI presents both a challenge and an opportunity for organizations that are balancing decades-old infrastructure with the demands of contemporary business operations. Many enterprises, especially those operating in sectors like finance, manufacturing, and government, rely on legacy applications that were developed long before modern APIs and standardized communication protocols became prevalent. These systems often perform critical functions and store valuable data, making it impractical to replace them outright. Instead, businesses seek to extend the lifespan of these systems by connecting them to modern messaging environments through MAPI.

Legacy systems typically lack the native ability to interface directly with modern messaging servers like Microsoft Exchange. They were often designed in closed architectures using proprietary data formats, standalone databases, or older communication protocols that do not align with today's standards. MAPI offers a robust solution by providing a bridge between these legacy platforms and contemporary messaging services, enabling legacy applications to send notifications, generate automated reports via email, and integrate with workflows that rely on Exchange-based communication.

The integration process begins with understanding the capabilities and limitations of the legacy system. Some older applications may already support basic email functionality via SMTP or other simple protocols, but MAPI provides a deeper level of integration. By leveraging MAPI, organizations can enable legacy systems to create fully formatted messages with rich text, attachments, and custom metadata, as well as interact with calendars, contacts, and task management features present in modern messaging platforms.

A common scenario in legacy integration is connecting enterprise resource planning (ERP) systems, customer relationship management (CRM) software, or custom-built mainframe applications to Exchange through a middleware layer that communicates via MAPI. This middleware acts as an intermediary, translating data and commands from the legacy application into MAPI calls. For example, a manufacturing system that tracks inventory levels might trigger the middleware to generate a MAPI-based email alert to supply chain managers when stock levels fall below a certain threshold. The middleware would use MAPI to create and send a message with relevant data, such as the product ID, location, and reorder requirements, directly into the managers' inboxes or shared mailboxes.

One of the core benefits of using MAPI in this context is its ability to access more than just email functionality. Legacy systems can be enhanced to interact with public folders for information sharing, schedule tasks through calendar objects, or update contact lists in the Exchange address book. This allows older applications to become part of larger, automated workflows that span across multiple departments and communication channels.

Security is a critical concern when integrating legacy systems with modern frameworks like MAPI. Many older applications were built at a time when security threats were far less sophisticated, meaning they often lack support for modern encryption protocols and authentication mechanisms. When integrating such systems with MAPI, it is essential to enforce secure communication through SSL/TLS and restrict access through role-based permissions within Active Directory. By configuring MAPI to require authenticated sessions and ensuring the middleware or integration layer operates under tightly controlled service accounts, organizations can minimize security risks while extending legacy system functionality.

Another key consideration is the handling of data formats. Legacy applications frequently store information in non-standard or proprietary formats that do not map directly to MAPI properties or modern messaging standards. The integration process must include data transformation logic to convert legacy data into formats that MAPI and Exchange can interpret correctly. This may involve scripting, custom development, or the use of integration platforms that provide mapping tools to translate legacy data structures into MIME-compliant messages or calendar appointments recognized by Exchange.

Performance optimization is also an important factor when integrating legacy systems with MAPI. Legacy systems may not have been designed with the performance demands of modern environments in mind. Generating large volumes of automated emails or processing high-frequency triggers can strain older systems and affect messaging throughput. To address this, middleware can be configured to batch process events, prioritize critical communications, and manage retries to balance system load. Additionally, MAPI's asynchronous capabilities allow integration layers to perform background processing, queuing messages for delivery without overloading the legacy application's core functionality.

Integrating legacy systems with MAPI also provides significant opportunities for business process improvement. By connecting older systems to modern messaging environments, organizations can automate previously manual tasks, reduce operational silos, and enhance collaboration across departments. For example, a financial system from the early 2000s might generate paper-based or standalone reports, but when integrated with MAPI, it can automatically email financial summaries to accounting teams, archive records in public folders, and even trigger meeting invitations to discuss financial discrepancies.

Organizations undertaking legacy integration projects with MAPI must also focus on monitoring and maintenance. Since legacy applications may not natively provide diagnostic logs or error handling mechanisms that align with modern IT practices, it is essential to implement comprehensive monitoring solutions. Logging MAPI transactions, tracking message delivery status, and alerting IT teams to failures or bottlenecks ensures that integrated systems remain reliable and that issues are addressed before they impact critical business functions.

The long-term success of integrating legacy systems with MAPI depends on careful planning and incremental execution. Businesses must evaluate the strategic value of each legacy system, prioritize integrations that deliver the greatest operational benefits, and remain adaptable to evolving technology landscapes. While modern cloud-based APIs and services continue to gain traction, MAPI's flexibility and deep integration capabilities make it a valuable asset for organizations looking to modernize without abandoning their legacy investments.

By bridging the gap between legacy platforms and modern communication infrastructures, MAPI empowers organizations to extract greater value from their existing systems, reduce operational inefficiencies, and build communication workflows that support today's agile and interconnected business environments. This approach extends the functional lifespan of critical legacy applications while ensuring alignment with contemporary security standards, user expectations, and regulatory compliance requirements.

MAPI vs. Other Communication Protocols

In the realm of enterprise messaging and business communications, multiple protocols have emerged to handle the exchange of messages and related data. Among them, the Messaging Application Programming Interface, or MAPI, stands out for its deep integration with Microsoft Exchange and its ability to provide comprehensive access to messaging functions beyond simple email transmission. To fully appreciate the role and value of MAPI, it is necessary to examine how it compares with other widely used communication protocols such as SMTP, POP3, IMAP, and modern RESTful APIs like Microsoft Graph.

MAPI was designed by Microsoft as a complete framework that offers client applications full access to the features of messaging servers. Unlike protocols that primarily focus on the transport and retrieval of messages, MAPI enables applications to interact with message stores, address books, calendars, and task lists. It allows for advanced operations such as creating custom message stores, managing public folders, and subscribing to event notifications. This makes MAPI a robust solution for enterprises that require tight coupling between their messaging systems and business applications.

In contrast, SMTP, the Simple Mail Transfer Protocol, is designed solely for sending emails between servers. SMTP is a transport-layer protocol that plays a crucial role in delivering email messages over the internet, but it does not provide functionality for retrieving or managing messages once they reach the recipient's mailbox. SMTP is widely used in both personal and business settings because of its simplicity and ubiquity, but it is limited to outbound message delivery. Applications using SMTP for email dispatch still need to rely on other protocols or interfaces for additional functionality such as inbox management, calendar scheduling, or address book access.

POP3, or Post Office Protocol version 3, provides basic functionality for retrieving messages from a mail server. It was designed for offline mail access, where users download their emails to a local device and then delete them from the server. POP3 is a straightforward and lightweight protocol, making it well-suited for early email clients and environments where bandwidth was a concern. However, in modern business scenarios, POP3's limitations become apparent. It lacks synchronization capabilities, meaning that changes made on one device, such as reading or deleting an email, do not reflect on other devices. This is a significant drawback in today's multi-device work environments where users expect seamless synchronization across desktops, laptops, smartphones, and tablets.

IMAP, or Internet Message Access Protocol, addresses many of POP3's shortcomings by allowing clients to manage messages directly on the server. With IMAP, users can view message headers, organize messages into folders, and synchronize read/unread statuses across multiple devices. IMAP has become a popular choice for businesses seeking lightweight and efficient email synchronization across distributed teams and mobile workforces. Despite its advantages over POP3, IMAP remains focused primarily on message retrieval and management. It does not natively support access to calendars, contacts, or other collaborative features, which are essential for integrated enterprise communication systems.

This is where MAPI distinguishes itself most significantly. By offering not just email capabilities but also integration with calendars, tasks, notes, public folders, and address books, MAPI supports the broader collaboration requirements of modern organizations. It allows client applications like Microsoft Outlook to deliver a unified interface where employees can manage all aspects of their workday, from scheduling meetings to accessing shared resources and automating workflows. MAPI's event notification system allows applications to monitor changes in message stores, providing real-time updates and supporting automation scenarios that are difficult to achieve with protocols like IMAP or POP3.

Another area where MAPI offers an advantage is its extensibility. With Extended MAPI, developers can build custom service providers, create bespoke workflows, and extend the platform to support unique business needs. For example, enterprises can create transport providers that route messages through specialized communication systems or build message store providers that integrate with proprietary databases. This level of extensibility is not present in protocols such as SMTP, POP3, or IMAP, which follow more rigid standards focused on core messaging functions.

Despite its powerful capabilities, MAPI is not always the most appropriate choice for every situation. Its tight integration with Microsoft Exchange means it is best suited for organizations that rely heavily on Microsoft ecosystems. For businesses using alternative mail servers, cloud-based services, or lightweight messaging needs, simpler protocols such as SMTP or IMAP may be more efficient and easier to implement. Additionally, MAPI typically requires a more complex setup, including managing service providers, configuring sessions, and ensuring proper security settings. For smaller organizations or applications that only need basic email-sending capabilities, SMTP might provide a quicker and less resource-intensive solution.

The rise of RESTful APIs, particularly Microsoft Graph API, has also reshaped the landscape. Microsoft Graph offers developers a unified endpoint to access not only email, calendars, and contacts but also SharePoint, Teams, OneDrive, and other Microsoft 365 services. Unlike MAPI, which operates using binary protocols and COM-based libraries, Graph leverages modern web standards such as HTTP and JSON, making it easier to integrate with cloud-native applications and web services. Graph provides flexibility for developers building cross-platform and mobile-first applications that need to interact with Microsoft 365 services without depending on traditional Windows-based infrastructure.

Nonetheless, MAPI still holds a critical role in many enterprises, especially in on-premises or hybrid environments where Exchange Server remains a core component of IT infrastructure. In such settings, MAPI enables organizations to achieve deeper integration with Exchange features that RESTful APIs may not fully replicate, such as custom message stores, advanced delegate access configurations, and fine-grained control over Outlook profiles.

Ultimately, the choice between MAPI and other communication protocols depends on the specific requirements of the business and the technical landscape in which it operates. MAPI excels in environments where comprehensive integration with Exchange is necessary, and where business applications must interact with a wide range of collaborative features beyond simple email delivery. Protocols like SMTP, POP3, and IMAP remain highly relevant for their intended purposes, offering lightweight and reliable solutions for email transport and retrieval. Meanwhile, modern APIs like Microsoft Graph continue to expand the possibilities for cloud-first development and integrated service delivery.

Each protocol has its strengths and weaknesses, and in many enterprise environments, a combination of these technologies is used to address different aspects of business communication. MAPI's enduring presence in corporate IT ecosystems highlights its unique ability to bridge messaging systems with broader business processes, while other protocols continue to provide the foundational transport mechanisms that underpin global email infrastructure.

The Role of MAPI in Enterprise Messaging

MAPI, or Messaging Application Programming Interface, plays a pivotal role in enterprise messaging systems by acting as the primary mechanism that allows applications to interact directly with email servers, particularly Microsoft Exchange. In the corporate environment, where email remains one of the most critical tools for internal and external communication, MAPI ensures that users and applications have access to a wide array of messaging features that go far beyond the simple sending and receiving of emails. Its deep integration with collaboration tools and business workflows has made it an essential component of enterprise IT infrastructure for decades.

At its core, MAPI provides a set of APIs that allow client applications, most notably Microsoft Outlook, to connect to and manage messaging servers. Unlike protocols such as SMTP or IMAP that are limited to the transport or retrieval of messages, MAPI grants full access to the messaging system's internal objects. This includes emails, calendar items, contacts, tasks, notes, and public folders. By offering such a broad scope of functionality, MAPI enables enterprises to implement unified communication platforms where all aspects of professional correspondence and collaboration are consolidated into a single interface.

The integration of MAPI with Microsoft Exchange allows businesses to create tightly coordinated environments where users can manage their entire workflow without switching between disparate tools. A typical enterprise relies heavily on calendars to schedule meetings, reserve resources, and coordinate with internal and external stakeholders. Through MAPI, client applications can interact programmatically with calendar objects, allowing users to send and receive meeting invitations, check attendee availability, reserve conference rooms, and even create recurring appointments that sync across devices. This seamless calendar management is one of the key reasons enterprises adopt MAPI in environments where collaboration is central to business operations.

MAPI also plays a critical role in enabling advanced mailbox features that businesses depend on for productivity and security. For example, it facilitates the implementation of delegate access, which allows executives to grant administrative assistants the ability to manage their email and calendar on their behalf. Through MAPI, permissions can be configured so that assistants can send emails, accept meeting requests, and organize schedules while maintaining clear visibility into who is acting on behalf of whom. This kind of delegation is essential in large organizations where hierarchical workflows and role-based access controls are commonplace.

In enterprise messaging, reliability and consistency are paramount. MAPI provides robust session management and transaction control, ensuring that operations such as sending messages, moving emails between folders, or updating calendar events are processed reliably even under high user loads. The client-server model that underpins MAPI operations ensures that client applications remain synchronized with the server, maintaining consistency across user devices and preventing data conflicts. In environments where thousands of employees might be accessing the same messaging infrastructure, this consistency is essential for avoiding operational disruptions.

Security is another domain where MAPI plays a vital role in enterprise messaging. As part of its deep integration with Microsoft Exchange, MAPI supports encryption, authentication, and access control mechanisms that are aligned with enterprise security policies. MAPI sessions are typically authenticated using Active Directory credentials, enabling single sign-on capabilities and reducing the administrative burden of managing multiple authentication systems. Furthermore, MAPI communications can be secured through transport encryption protocols like SSL/TLS, while S/MIME support enables message-level encryption and digital signatures to protect sensitive business communications.

MAPI's ability to integrate directly with other enterprise applications is one of its most valuable features. Many organizations develop custom applications or middleware that leverage MAPI to automate routine tasks and integrate messaging services into broader business processes. For instance, customer support systems can automatically generate MAPI-based emails when service tickets reach certain thresholds, or ERP systems can send inventory alerts and purchase order updates directly through Exchange. By embedding messaging functionality into line-of-business applications, enterprises can improve operational efficiency, reduce manual errors, and ensure that critical communications are delivered promptly to the right recipients.

The event-driven capabilities provided by MAPI further enhance its role in enterprise messaging. MAPI applications can subscribe to notifications that alert them to changes within the messaging environment, such as the arrival of a new email, the update of a calendar event, or modifications to shared folders. This allows businesses to build systems that react in real time to messaging events, automating workflows such as triggering alerts, initiating approval processes, or updating dashboards based on the latest communication data.

MAPI is also indispensable in managing public folders and shared mailboxes, which are commonly used by teams and departments to collaborate more effectively. Public folders provide shared access to emails, documents, and calendar items that are relevant to multiple users. Through MAPI, client applications can create, modify, and delete public folders, as well as control user permissions and synchronize changes across the organization. Shared mailboxes, often used by customer service teams or project groups, benefit from MAPI's ability to maintain folder structures, manage message flags, and track read/unread statuses consistently across all users who access the shared environment.

In hybrid environments where organizations maintain both on-premises Exchange servers and cloud-based Microsoft 365 services, MAPI continues to play a central role. MAPI over HTTP has modernized connectivity between client applications and Exchange servers, providing enhanced reliability and performance, particularly for remote workers. Even as organizations increasingly migrate to cloud-first strategies, MAPI remains integral to the smooth operation of hybrid deployments where legacy systems and modern services must coexist.

Despite the emergence of newer APIs such as Microsoft Graph, MAPI continues to be a cornerstone for many businesses that rely on on-premises or hybrid Exchange deployments. Its comprehensive API set, advanced integration options, and support for enterprise-specific features make it difficult to fully replace in certain complex environments. Enterprises that require granular control over Outlook profiles, message stores, and customized messaging workflows often continue to depend on MAPI for mission-critical operations.

MAPI's longstanding role in enterprise messaging reflects its unique ability to serve as a bridge between messaging systems and the broader landscape of business applications and processes. It supports not only day-to-day email communications but also the intricate workflows, security requirements, and collaboration needs of modern organizations. By offering direct access to the full functionality of enterprise messaging servers, MAPI continues to provide businesses with a reliable, flexible, and scalable foundation for communication and collaboration across the enterprise.

Streamlining Workflow Through MAPI Integration

The integration of MAPI into enterprise environments offers powerful capabilities to streamline workflows and eliminate inefficiencies that often plague business operations. As organizations expand and adopt more complex business processes, the need to automate communication and ensure that messaging systems are tightly coupled with operational workflows becomes more critical. MAPI, with its deep access to the full suite of messaging features in Microsoft Exchange, provides businesses with a versatile toolset to optimize these processes. Through MAPI integration, businesses can achieve higher levels of automation, improve cross-functional collaboration, and reduce manual tasks that slow down productivity.

At the core of workflow streamlining through MAPI is its ability to interact directly with various objects within the messaging ecosystem. These include emails, calendar appointments, tasks, contacts, and even public folders. This broad range of accessible elements allows organizations to create highly tailored workflows that align directly with their operational requirements. For instance, an organization can develop a system where a MAPI-enabled application automatically generates and sends follow-up emails to customers once a support ticket is closed, pulling relevant data from both the ticketing system and the message store. This reduces the need for manual intervention by customer service representatives and ensures consistent communication with clients.

MAPI integration also enhances approval workflows, a critical area in business processes where delays can have significant downstream impacts. In traditional environments, approvals for processes such as procurement, project milestones, or HR actions often rely on manual email chains or face-to-face meetings. By integrating MAPI with existing business applications like ERP or HR management systems, approvals can be automated and embedded directly within the messaging infrastructure. For example, when a purchase requisition exceeds a specific budget threshold, the ERP system can automatically trigger a MAPI-based email to the relevant manager's inbox, including pre-filled approval buttons or links. The manager's response can then be captured via MAPI, updating the ERP system in real time and advancing the workflow to the next stage without the need for additional manual processing.

Another key aspect of streamlining workflows through MAPI integration is the automation of notifications and alerts. Many business processes require timely updates to ensure stakeholders are informed of critical developments. Whether it is a missed project deadline, a system failure, or the completion of a key deliverable, MAPI enables business systems to send automated alerts directly to user inboxes or team mailboxes. Because MAPI allows access to distribution lists and shared mailboxes via the address book provider, notifications can be intelligently routed based on predefined rules, such as sending a high-priority alert to all members of the operations team or escalating critical issues to senior management automatically.

Document management workflows also benefit greatly from MAPI integration. In industries where regulatory compliance is paramount, such as finance, healthcare, and legal, documents must often pass through several review and approval stages before finalization. MAPI can be integrated with document management systems to automate the distribution and tracking of these documents. For instance, when a new contract draft is uploaded to a secure repository, a MAPI-based workflow could generate a message to all relevant reviewers with the document attached or linked, include a deadline for feedback, and set automatic reminders. Reviewers' comments and approvals can be collected and logged via integrated messaging responses, ensuring a seamless and auditable process.

Beyond traditional email, MAPI also supports interaction with calendar objects, opening up further opportunities for workflow automation. Calendar-based workflows can be streamlined by automatically scheduling meetings, allocating resources, or sending reminders based on business events. A project management application, for example, can leverage MAPI to automatically book project status meetings once a milestone is completed or to update shared calendars with new deadlines and deliverable dates. This automation not only saves time but also ensures that key personnel remain aligned with project timelines without the need for repetitive, manual calendar management tasks.

MAPI's property model, which allows developers to customize metadata for messaging objects, further enhances workflow efficiency. Custom properties can be used to tag messages with workflow-specific information, such as project codes, client IDs, or escalation levels. These custom tags can then be leveraged by automated rules to drive workflow decisions, such as routing messages to different teams based on project codes or flagging emails for priority processing based on escalation indicators. This level of customization allows organizations to tailor workflows to their unique operational structures and objectives, ensuring optimal alignment with business processes.

The ability to subscribe to notifications using MAPI's event-driven capabilities is another factor in streamlining workflows. Applications can be configured to listen for specific changes within the message store or address book, such as the arrival of new messages in a designated folder or the modification of contact details. This real-time event monitoring allows workflows to respond immediately to changes, triggering subsequent actions such as initiating approval processes, forwarding critical messages to specialized teams, or generating automated reports.

In large enterprises where workflows often span multiple departments and business units, MAPI integration supports the orchestration of cross-functional processes. By enabling different systems to interact with a centralized messaging platform, MAPI helps eliminate operational silos and ensures that information flows freely and efficiently between teams. For example, an integrated sales and operations workflow might involve automatically notifying the production team when a sales order reaches a certain status in the CRM system. Through MAPI, this notification can be enriched with relevant data such as customer details, delivery schedules, and product specifications, all consolidated into a structured message that triggers follow-up actions downstream.

Security and compliance are embedded in MAPI-based workflows, ensuring that all automated communications adhere to enterprise policies. MAPI works in concert with Exchange security features, including access controls, encryption, and message journaling, to ensure that sensitive information is only accessible to authorized users and that workflow-related communications are fully auditable. Automated encryption and digital signing of messages can be integrated into workflows to meet industry-specific compliance standards without burdening users with additional manual steps.

By reducing the reliance on manual communication tasks and embedding messaging capabilities directly into business systems, MAPI integration not only streamlines workflows but also reduces the risk of human error, accelerates decision-making processes, and increases overall productivity. It transforms email from a passive communication channel into an active component of automated business operations, creating a more responsive and agile enterprise environment where workflows are seamlessly driven by real-time data and automated messaging triggers.

Advanced MAPI Functionality for Business

MAPI, or Messaging Application Programming Interface, is often associated with the basic functions of sending and receiving emails or managing calendar appointments within Microsoft Outlook. However, the advanced features of MAPI provide businesses with a far more extensive toolkit, enabling organizations to unlock new levels of productivity, security, and integration. These advanced capabilities are particularly relevant for enterprises that require deeper control over their messaging infrastructure and more sophisticated automation across workflows.

One of the most powerful aspects of MAPI is its ability to manage and manipulate message stores in a highly customized way. Through Extended MAPI, applications gain access to low-level functions that allow them to create and manage custom message stores and folders. This gives organizations the ability to organize data beyond the default mailbox hierarchy. For example, businesses can develop custom folders that act as repositories for automated reports, compliance-related communications, or project-specific correspondence, all within the existing Exchange environment. These folders can be created dynamically through code, allowing applications to adapt in real time as business requirements evolve.

Advanced MAPI functionality also extends to transport and routing customization. While most messaging systems rely on Exchange's native transport services to move messages between servers and clients, MAPI allows for the creation of custom transport providers. These providers can be programmed to reroute messages based on specific criteria such as recipient domain, message type, or business rules defined by the organization. For instance, an enterprise could create a MAPI-based solution that automatically directs internal compliance emails to an archiving system while routing customer-facing messages through an alternative secure gateway. This granular control over transport paths is critical for businesses operating under strict regulatory frameworks or with highly segmented communication workflows.

Another key area where advanced MAPI functionality proves invaluable is in security and access control. MAPI allows for fine-grained permissions management, making it possible to implement advanced delegation and mailbox access scenarios. In large organizations, executives often require administrative assistants or team members to manage their email and calendars on their behalf. With MAPI, businesses can programmatically assign delegate permissions at varying levels of granularity, from full mailbox access to more limited permissions such as calendar-only or task management access. These permissions can be adjusted automatically through business applications based on role changes, project assignments, or organizational restructuring, ensuring that access rights are always aligned with business needs.

The notification and event-driven features of MAPI play a significant role in enabling real-time business automation. Applications can subscribe to a variety of events within the messaging infrastructure, such as the creation, modification, or deletion of messages, appointments, or tasks. This capability allows for the construction of responsive business processes that react immediately to changes in the messaging system. A financial institution, for example, could use MAPI to automatically flag and escalate any incoming messages containing sensitive transaction data, triggering alerts to compliance officers and initiating an audit trail. Similarly, sales teams could leverage event-driven MAPI functionality to receive instant notifications when a key client sends a time-sensitive request, reducing response times and improving customer service.

MAPI's advanced handling of message properties and custom metadata further enhances its business value. Beyond standard properties like subject, sender, and recipients, MAPI supports the creation of custom properties that applications can attach to messages, contacts, and calendar items. These properties can carry essential business-specific data such as project codes, approval status, workflow stages, or custom tags required for regulatory compliance. By leveraging this functionality, organizations can enable applications to filter, categorize, and process messages based on highly specific business rules. This facilitates the creation of intelligent automation systems that classify and prioritize incoming communications, reducing manual intervention and improving efficiency.

Another advanced feature is MAPI's integration with public folders and shared mailboxes, which are critical for supporting collaborative workflows. Public folders are often used to share documents, email threads, and calendar items between teams or departments. With MAPI, developers can build solutions that automatically create and manage public folders based on project lifecycles or organizational hierarchies. For instance, when a new project is initiated, a custom MAPI application could automatically set up a shared mailbox and related public folders, assign permissions to the project team, and configure notifications to track new items added to the shared resources. This eliminates administrative overhead and ensures that collaborative spaces are consistently configured across the organization.

Advanced MAPI functionality also includes the ability to build custom Outlook forms and user interface extensions. MAPI provides the foundation for creating tailored user experiences within Outlook by allowing organizations to design custom forms for specific business workflows. For example, a legal department could use MAPI to create a specialized form within Outlook for contract approval requests, including custom fields for client names, contract types, and risk assessments. These forms can integrate directly with backend systems, automatically populating databases, triggering document workflows, or generating audit logs based on user input.

Integration with external systems is another area where MAPI shines. Through its extensible API, MAPI allows organizations to link their messaging infrastructure with CRM, ERP, document management systems, and other business applications. A manufacturing company might develop a solution where production issues flagged in an ERP system automatically generate a detailed email with attachments sent via MAPI to the quality assurance team. The message could include production batch numbers, defect reports, and inspection results, providing all necessary data within a single, automatically generated communication. This level of integration streamlines cross-functional processes and ensures that teams have the information they need at their fingertips.

MAPI's ability to manage and manipulate Outlook profiles programmatically is another advanced capability that benefits businesses, especially during large-scale deployments or migrations. IT administrators can use MAPI to automate the creation and configuration of Outlook profiles across hundreds or thousands of user devices, reducing setup time and ensuring consistency in configuration. This is particularly valuable during Exchange upgrades, Office 365 migrations, or when deploying virtual desktop infrastructure environments where standardization is critical.

The performance optimization features available through MAPI also contribute to its value in business environments. Developers and administrators can fine-tune how MAPI handles large message stores, manages caching, and performs background synchronization tasks. This level of control is important for organizations with high-volume mailboxes, such as customer support centers or legal teams managing large amounts of documentation via email. By optimizing MAPI operations, businesses can improve application responsiveness, reduce latency, and maintain optimal user experiences even in demanding environments.

Advanced MAPI functionality transforms business messaging from a simple communication tool into a dynamic platform for automation, integration, and process optimization. Its extensive feature set empowers organizations to build highly customized and efficient workflows, maintain strict control over messaging security, and automate complex tasks that would otherwise require significant manual effort. As businesses increasingly seek ways to enhance productivity and align communication systems with core operations, MAPI continues to provide the technical foundation needed to meet these evolving demands.

Leveraging MAPI for CRM Systems

Customer Relationship Management systems are central to how businesses manage their interactions with clients, prospects, and partners. A CRM system serves as the nerve center for organizing customer data, tracking sales opportunities, managing support requests, and driving marketing initiatives. Yet, the true power of a CRM platform is realized when it is fully integrated with an organization's communication infrastructure. Leveraging MAPI, or Messaging Application Programming Interface, provides businesses with an opportunity to create seamless interactions between their CRM systems and enterprise messaging environments, most notably Microsoft Exchange and Outlook. The result is a more cohesive and automated process that enhances the efficiency of customer engagement workflows.

MAPI plays a critical role in extending CRM capabilities by bridging communication data with customer records. One of the most impactful uses of MAPI in CRM integration is the automation of email tracking and logging. In many organizations, customer-facing employees such as sales representatives, account managers, or support agents rely heavily on email correspondence to engage with customers. However, manually copying emails into the CRM or associating them with customer records is both time-consuming and prone to error. By integrating MAPI with the CRM system, emails can be automatically captured, categorized, and linked to the relevant customer profiles within the CRM database. This ensures that all communication history is preserved, providing a complete view of the client relationship for all stakeholders.

Beyond basic email logging, MAPI allows for the enrichment of CRM records through metadata extraction. MAPI's access to message properties such as sender, recipients, subject, timestamps, and custom fields enables organizations to extract critical information and map it to CRM fields automatically. For instance, emails from high-value customers can be flagged and prioritized based on data pulled directly from the message headers or contents, triggering workflows within the CRM system such as alerting account managers or initiating follow-up tasks. This level of integration not only streamlines communication processes but also ensures that no important customer interaction is overlooked.

Calendar synchronization is another valuable function enabled by MAPI when integrated with CRM platforms. Customer-facing teams often schedule meetings, calls, and events both within Outlook and the CRM system. Without integration, maintaining consistency between these two environments requires manual updates, leading to discrepancies and missed appointments. Through MAPI, CRM systems can programmatically create and update calendar events directly in users' Exchange mailboxes. This allows meetings scheduled within the CRM to automatically appear in users' Outlook calendars, complete with details such as client names, meeting agendas, and location information. Likewise, meetings created in Outlook can be automatically pushed back to the CRM system, ensuring alignment across all platforms and eliminating the risk of double-booking or incomplete scheduling data.

MAPI integration also enhances task and activity management within CRM systems. Sales representatives and customer service agents often rely on a combination of CRM tasks and Outlook task lists to manage their daily responsibilities. By using MAPI, organizations can synchronize CRM tasks with Outlook's task manager, enabling users to view, update, and complete their CRM-related activities directly from within Outlook. This seamless integration promotes user adoption by allowing employees to work within familiar interfaces while ensuring that task completion and status updates are automatically reflected in the CRM system. As a result, productivity increases, and reporting accuracy is improved since managers can rely on up-to-date information on task progress and completion rates.

Advanced MAPI features also support the automation of follow-up communication within CRM workflows. A common scenario in sales and customer service involves creating templated follow-up emails after meetings, service tickets, or project milestones. MAPI enables CRM systems to automate this process by generating customized email drafts in Outlook, pre-populated with client details, meeting notes, and next steps. Users can review and personalize these drafts before sending them, maintaining a personal touch while ensuring that follow-up communication happens consistently and without delay.

Leveraging MAPI for CRM integration further supports customer data protection and regulatory compliance efforts. In industries such as finance, healthcare, and legal services, it is vital that all client communications are captured, encrypted, and stored according to strict regulatory requirements. MAPI, in conjunction with Exchange's security and compliance features, allows CRM systems to automatically archive emails, enforce retention policies, and apply encryption to sensitive messages. Additionally, through MAPI's event notification system, CRM applications can be alerted in real time when key communications occur, enabling immediate logging and escalation of critical client interactions.

MAPI also plays a role in facilitating more advanced CRM use cases, such as sales pipeline automation and customer support escalation. For example, a CRM system can use MAPI to monitor specific folders within users' mailboxes, such as a shared inbox for incoming sales inquiries or support requests. When new messages arrive, MAPI can trigger workflows within the CRM to automatically create leads, cases, or tickets and assign them to the appropriate teams based on predefined rules. This level of automation eliminates the bottleneck of manual data entry and accelerates response times, ensuring that customer inquiries are handled efficiently and effectively.

In addition to back-end automation, MAPI enhances the user experience by enabling tighter integration between CRM data and the Outlook user interface. With MAPI's ability to access address books and contact lists, CRM systems can display contextual customer data directly within Outlook when users interact with emails or calendar events. For instance, when a salesperson opens an email from a client, the CRM could surface key data such as open opportunities, recent support tickets, or outstanding invoices right inside the Outlook pane. This empowers users with real-time insights and helps them make informed decisions without switching between applications.

The scalability of MAPI further ensures that CRM integrations can grow alongside business needs. Whether an organization has a handful of users or thousands across multiple regions, MAPI provides the flexibility to automate communication processes at scale. Batch processing of emails, tasks, and calendar events can be implemented to support large volumes of interactions without compromising system performance. This scalability is crucial for global enterprises that rely on CRM systems to manage complex customer relationships across multiple departments and time zones.

By integrating MAPI with CRM systems, businesses create a dynamic and connected environment where customer interactions are seamlessly captured, managed, and acted upon within both the messaging and CRM platforms. This not only boosts operational efficiency but also enhances customer satisfaction by ensuring timely and personalized responses. MAPI becomes a key enabler in building a unified customer engagement strategy, aligning sales, marketing, and service efforts around a shared, real-time view of client communications and history.

MAPI in ERP and Financial Platforms

The integration of MAPI into ERP and financial platforms has become an increasingly valuable strategy for organizations looking to streamline communication, enhance process automation, and improve reporting accuracy within complex financial environments. ERP systems, which serve as the backbone for managing a company's resources, accounting functions, and supply chain processes, rely heavily on timely and accurate communication to ensure seamless business operations. By embedding MAPI into these systems, businesses gain the ability to automate email-based workflows, integrate financial alerts with messaging systems, and create real-time collaboration between financial data and enterprise communication tools like Microsoft Exchange.

At its core, MAPI provides the foundational layer that allows ERP and financial platforms to interface directly with an organization's messaging infrastructure. Instead of relying on external or manual processes to handle financial documents, alerts, and transaction confirmations, MAPI enables ERP systems to automatically generate and distribute this information via email. For example, financial documents such as purchase orders, invoices, payment confirmations, and account statements can be created and sent directly from the ERP platform to internal stakeholders, suppliers, or clients. MAPI's deep integration with Exchange ensures that these emails are delivered securely and that relevant data, including attachments and metadata, are properly formatted and tracked throughout the communication process.

One of the most impactful use cases for MAPI within ERP systems is the automation of financial alerts. Businesses often need to send timely notifications regarding critical financial events such as payment due dates, budget overruns, cash flow discrepancies, or unauthorized transactions. Without MAPI, these alerts might require manual intervention or third-party tools to be communicated effectively. However, with MAPI integrated into the ERP system, alerts can be automatically generated and sent to the appropriate individuals or teams. For example, if a payment from a key client fails to process or if an invoice is overdue, MAPI can trigger an automated message to the accounts receivable team, along with the client's contact details and a copy of the original invoice. This level of automation minimizes response times and ensures that financial issues are addressed promptly.

MAPI also enhances financial approval workflows by connecting ERP systems with the calendaring and messaging capabilities of Microsoft Outlook. In large organizations, financial decisions such as approving purchase orders, vendor contracts, or capital expenditures often require multi-tiered approval chains. By leveraging MAPI, ERP systems can automate the generation of approval requests, sending emails with embedded approval options to managers and executives directly through their Outlook inboxes. The responses to these requests can be programmatically captured via MAPI and recorded back into the ERP system, updating the status of the approval in real time. This integration eliminates the need for paper-based approvals or disjointed workflows that rely on manual tracking, significantly reducing bottlenecks and ensuring a smooth financial authorization process.

Another critical function that MAPI brings to ERP and financial platforms is the integration of financial reporting with enterprise messaging. Monthly, quarterly, and annual financial reports are essential tools for leadership teams to assess performance, make strategic decisions, and ensure regulatory compliance. With MAPI, ERP systems can automate the generation and distribution of these reports to designated recipients. The reports can be attached as PDF, Excel, or CSV files within an automatically generated email, accompanied by executive summaries or key highlights within the body of the message. Advanced implementations may even leverage MAPI's capabilities to send reports to public folders or shared mailboxes, ensuring that teams have centralized and controlled access to important financial documentation.

Beyond basic email communication, MAPI also supports the creation of event-driven workflows within ERP and financial systems. For example, when inventory levels in the ERP system fall below a critical threshold, MAPI can trigger a notification to the procurement team along with a system-generated purchase requisition. Alternatively, if a vendor contract is approaching its renewal date, MAPI can automate the process of notifying both the contract owner and the legal department, while simultaneously scheduling review meetings directly in their Outlook calendars. By tying ERP-generated events to messaging and scheduling functions through MAPI, organizations reduce the risk of operational oversights and ensure that financial processes stay aligned with business objectives.

Financial platforms integrated with MAPI can also benefit from enhanced audit trails and compliance monitoring. In highly regulated industries, documenting financial communications is essential for passing audits and meeting legal requirements. MAPI enables ERP systems to automatically archive all financial messages, including supporting documents and approval responses, into secure storage or compliance systems. Additionally, custom properties can be added to emails through MAPI to tag them with compliance-related information such as transaction IDs, regulatory codes, or audit case numbers. This level of detail ensures that financial communication records are easily searchable and properly aligned with compliance frameworks such as SOX, GDPR, or industry-specific regulations.

MAPI's ability to interact with address books and contact directories further enhances ERP and financial operations. By accessing the organization's Active Directory or Global Address List via MAPI, ERP systems can validate recipient email addresses and ensure that financial communications are sent to the correct stakeholders. This minimizes the risk of misdirected emails and enhances data security by reducing the chance of sensitive financial information being shared with unauthorized individuals. Additionally, ERP systems can leverage MAPI to dynamically select distribution lists based on business rules, such as routing payment notifications to regional finance teams or sending project-related budget alerts to specific project managers.

Advanced MAPI functionality also supports ERP-driven escalation processes. For example, if a financial transaction exceeds a predefined risk threshold or triggers an internal control exception, MAPI can be used to automatically escalate the issue by sending emails to senior finance executives or compliance officers, complete with contextual data and supporting documentation. Escalations can be prioritized and flagged according to severity, leveraging MAPI's ability to set email importance levels and integrate with Outlook's rules engine.

Integrating MAPI into ERP and financial platforms transforms how organizations manage financial communication and approvals, making these processes faster, more secure, and fully traceable. It reduces manual workload by embedding messaging capabilities directly into critical financial workflows, allowing teams to focus on value-added activities such as analysis and strategic planning. From automating alerts and approvals to generating comprehensive financial reports and maintaining compliance, MAPI delivers a robust and versatile solution that enhances the operational efficiency and accuracy of financial systems across the enterprise.

Data Security and Compliance in MAPI Communications

As organizations continue to rely heavily on MAPI to facilitate messaging and collaboration within enterprise environments, the focus on data security and compliance becomes increasingly critical. MAPI, as a messaging API, provides deep access to sensitive business data such as emails, contacts, calendar events, tasks, and confidential documents. This access, while enabling seamless communication and workflow automation, also introduces a range of security and compliance considerations that must be addressed to protect the organization's assets and meet regulatory obligations.

Data security in MAPI communications begins with secure authentication and access control. Since MAPI is tightly integrated with Microsoft Exchange and, by extension, Active Directory, it inherits the authentication and authorization mechanisms provided by these systems. User credentials are validated through Active Directory, and access permissions are enforced based on predefined security groups and role-based access controls. This integration ensures that only authorized users and applications can establish MAPI sessions and interact with mailbox data. In high-security environments, multi-factor authentication is commonly implemented, adding an additional layer of identity verification before granting access to MAPI-enabled systems.

The security of data in transit is another fundamental component of MAPI communication. MAPI over HTTP, the modern transport protocol for MAPI, leverages industry-standard encryption protocols such as SSL and TLS to secure all communication between client applications and Exchange servers. By encrypting data packets during transit, MAPI over HTTP mitigates the risk of interception by malicious actors attempting to eavesdrop on network traffic. For organizations that operate in highly regulated sectors such as finance, healthcare, and government, transport-level encryption is a baseline requirement to safeguard sensitive client data and proprietary information from unauthorized access during transmission.

Beyond securing the communication channel itself, MAPI also supports end-to-end message security through integration with S/MIME, or Secure/Multipurpose Internet Mail Extensions. S/MIME allows for individual messages to be encrypted and digitally signed, ensuring that only intended recipients can decrypt and read the content. Additionally, digital signatures verify the authenticity of the sender and the integrity of the message, providing assurance that the content has not been tampered with in transit. Within MAPI-enabled environments, organizations can configure policies that enforce S/MIME encryption on sensitive emails, such as those containing financial records, legal documents, or personal identifiable information (PII).

Compliance plays an equally important role in MAPI communications, as organizations must adhere to a growing array of regulatory frameworks that govern how data is handled, stored, and shared. Regulations such as GDPR, HIPAA, SOX, and others impose strict rules on the confidentiality, integrity, and availability of sensitive data. MAPI integration with Exchange allows organizations to implement compliance controls directly within their messaging workflows. For example, data loss prevention (DLP) policies can be enforced to automatically scan outgoing messages for sensitive content such as credit card numbers, social security numbers, or confidential financial information. If a policy violation is detected, MAPI-enabled systems can trigger actions such as blocking message delivery, applying encryption, or notifying compliance officers for further review.

Archiving and retention policies are additional compliance mechanisms supported through MAPI communications. Many industries require that emails and associated metadata be retained for specific periods to meet legal and regulatory obligations. MAPI allows administrators to programmatically manage message retention within mailboxes, public folders, and shared mailboxes. Messages can be automatically moved to archive folders based on business rules, flagged for retention, or tagged with metadata that identifies them as subject to regulatory audits. These automated processes help organizations meet their legal requirements without relying on manual intervention, reducing the risk of accidental deletion or non-compliance.

Audit trails are another essential component of compliance within MAPI environments. Through MAPI's deep integration with Exchange, organizations can enable mailbox auditing features that log detailed information about user and administrator actions. Activities such as message deletions, folder modifications, permission changes, and mailbox access events are recorded and stored for review by compliance and security teams. This audit trail provides organizations with critical visibility into how sensitive data is handled, helping to identify suspicious activity, support investigations, and demonstrate compliance during external audits.

In addition to native Exchange capabilities, MAPI allows for the integration of third-party compliance tools and security platforms. Many organizations leverage email security gateways, advanced threat protection services, and encryption appliances to supplement their internal controls. By incorporating MAPI into these solutions, businesses can create end-to-end security workflows that span multiple systems and touchpoints. For example, incoming and outgoing messages processed via MAPI can be routed through external DLP solutions for policy enforcement or passed through secure email gateways that perform deep content inspection and malware scanning before the messages are delivered to end users.

MAPI's support for custom metadata further enhances compliance management. Developers can use MAPI to attach compliance-related tags to messages and calendar items, such as regulatory codes, business unit identifiers, or sensitivity labels. These tags enable automated systems to apply appropriate handling procedures, such as escalating certain messages for executive review or ensuring that emails with specific tags are archived according to extended retention schedules. Custom metadata can also be leveraged in reporting and auditing tools to generate compliance reports and dashboards that provide insights into data handling practices across the organization.

Backup and disaster recovery strategies also benefit from MAPI's capabilities. By enabling automated backups of message stores, public folders, and shared mailboxes via MAPI, organizations ensure that critical communications are protected against data loss scenarios such as system failures, ransomware attacks, or accidental deletions. These backup processes can be configured to comply with business continuity requirements and ensure that archived messages are recoverable and verifiable when needed.

The combination of data security and compliance features in MAPI communications makes it a trusted solution for enterprises operating in complex regulatory environments. Its tight integration with enterprise directory services, encryption protocols, auditing mechanisms, and compliance frameworks ensures that sensitive messaging data is protected from end to end. As regulatory pressures continue to grow and cyber threats become increasingly sophisticated, MAPI remains a critical tool for organizations seeking to secure their communication channels while maintaining full compliance with industry standards and legal requirements. The ability to embed security and compliance into messaging workflows at such a granular level positions MAPI as a cornerstone in the enterprise strategy to manage risk, protect sensitive information, and uphold the trust of customers and regulatory bodies alike.

MAPI and Encryption: Protecting Business Data

In an era where data breaches and cyber threats continue to grow in frequency and sophistication, organizations must prioritize the protection of sensitive business communications. MAPI, or Messaging Application Programming Interface, serves as a critical component within enterprise messaging environments, and its integration with encryption protocols is essential for securing the vast amount of data that flows through modern communication systems. MAPI operates as the bridge between client applications and messaging servers like Microsoft Exchange, making it a key player in the protection of business emails, calendar events, contacts, and other collaborative data. Through encryption, MAPI ensures that this data remains confidential, integral, and secure both during transmission and when at rest.

The first layer of security in MAPI communication is transport-level encryption. With the widespread adoption of MAPI over HTTP, the transport protocol has been modernized to support encryption through Secure Sockets Layer (SSL) and Transport Layer Security (TLS). These protocols are designed to protect data as it travels across networks, preventing unauthorized interception or tampering during transmission. When a MAPI-enabled client application, such as Microsoft Outlook, communicates with an Exchange server, all data packets are encapsulated within an encrypted tunnel established by SSL or TLS. This guarantees that sensitive information, including the content of emails, attachments, authentication credentials, and metadata, cannot be easily intercepted or read by attackers on the network.

MAPI also plays an important role in supporting message-level encryption through integration with Secure/Multipurpose Internet Mail Extensions (S/MIME). S/MIME is a widely adopted standard that allows organizations to encrypt individual email messages and apply digital signatures, ensuring that only authorized recipients can read the contents and verify the sender's identity. Within a MAPI-enabled environment, users and applications can create S/MIME-protected messages directly from their client interfaces. When encryption is applied, the message body and any attachments are encrypted using the recipient's public key. Only the recipient's private key, securely stored on their device, can decrypt the message and render its contents readable. This provides a robust safeguard against unauthorized access, even if the message is intercepted after leaving the secure transport channel.

Digital signatures, another component of S/MIME, enhance data integrity and non-repudiation. By signing a message with the sender's private key, the recipient can verify that the message originated from the claimed sender and that the content has not been altered during transit. MAPI makes it possible to automate the application of digital signatures within business workflows, such as when sending contracts, financial reports, or other high-value documents. This automation ensures consistent use of digital signatures and reduces the risk of human error in applying security controls to outbound communications.

In addition to user-initiated encryption, MAPI facilitates the enforcement of organization-wide encryption policies. Many businesses configure their Exchange servers to apply encryption rules automatically to certain categories of messages based on content, recipients, or sensitivity labels. MAPI enables seamless integration with these policies by supporting the tagging and classification of emails within client applications and backend workflows. For instance, emails marked as confidential or internal-use-only may automatically trigger encryption and be routed through secure messaging gateways, all managed transparently within the MAPI session. This helps businesses maintain compliance with internal security policies and external regulatory requirements without relying solely on end-user discretion.

The protection of data at rest is another vital aspect of MAPI-enabled environments. While MAPI itself primarily facilitates data access and transmission, it works closely with Exchange Server's built-in security features to safeguard stored data. Exchange databases can be encrypted using technologies such as BitLocker, ensuring that mailbox data, public folders, and archive stores remain secure even if the physical storage media is compromised. MAPI sessions accessing these encrypted databases operate seamlessly, ensuring that encryption at rest does not hinder performance or user experience while maintaining high security standards.

Custom business applications that leverage Extended MAPI can also implement encryption within automated workflows. For example, an internal application that generates financial reports or client statements can use MAPI to compose emails and apply S/MIME encryption before automatically sending them to designated recipients. This level of automation ensures that sensitive information is consistently encrypted according to corporate policies, reducing the likelihood of data leaks caused by oversight or negligence.

MAPI's role in encryption extends to integration with third-party security platforms and encryption appliances. Businesses operating in highly regulated industries, such as healthcare, finance, and legal services, often deploy specialized encryption solutions that work in tandem with MAPI. These platforms may provide additional controls such as enforced key management, advanced encryption algorithms, or secure message portals. Through MAPI, client applications can route emails through these encryption platforms, ensuring end-to-end security for particularly sensitive communications. Additionally, MAPI-enabled workflows can integrate with data loss prevention (DLP) systems that automatically detect and respond to policy violations, applying encryption where needed or blocking messages from being sent altogether.

Encryption through MAPI also supports the growing need for secure mobile and remote work. With more employees accessing corporate messaging systems from outside traditional office networks, the risk of exposure to unsecured public networks has increased significantly. MAPI over HTTP, combined with SSL/TLS and S/MIME, ensures that communication remains encrypted regardless of where users are located. Mobile devices, laptops, and remote workstations all benefit from these protections, allowing employees to work securely from any location without sacrificing access to vital messaging and collaboration tools.

The evolving regulatory landscape further amplifies the importance of encryption in MAPI communications. Laws such as the General Data Protection Regulation (GDPR), the Health Insurance Portability and

Accountability Act (HIPAA), and the Sarbanes-Oxley Act (SOX) place strict requirements on how organizations handle sensitive data. Encryption, as facilitated by MAPI and associated technologies, is a key control in achieving compliance with these regulations. By encrypting both data in transit and data at rest, and by applying digital signatures to verify authenticity and integrity, businesses can demonstrate due diligence in protecting client information and proprietary data.

MAPI's integration with encryption technologies ensures that business data remains secure throughout its lifecycle, from creation to transmission and storage. It empowers organizations to build messaging systems that not only facilitate productivity but also prioritize the protection of sensitive information in an increasingly threat-prone digital landscape. By leveraging MAPI's encryption capabilities, businesses safeguard their reputation, build trust with clients and partners, and maintain compliance with global data protection standards, all while enabling seamless and efficient communication across the enterprise.

Troubleshooting Common MAPI Issues

In enterprise environments where MAPI serves as the backbone for messaging applications such as Microsoft Outlook, encountering technical issues is not uncommon. These issues can disrupt communication, delay business processes, and affect user productivity. Understanding how to troubleshoot common MAPI problems is essential for IT administrators, developers, and support teams responsible for maintaining stable and efficient messaging infrastructures. MAPI issues may arise from misconfigurations, client-server communication breakdowns, authentication failures, or compatibility mismatches, and resolving them often requires a methodical approach to identify and correct the underlying cause.

One of the most frequent MAPI-related issues occurs when client applications fail to connect to the Exchange server. This can manifest as an inability to open Outlook or synchronize mailboxes, often accompanied by error messages indicating that MAPI cannot establish a session. The root cause of this problem may lie in network connectivity issues, incorrect server settings, or problems with the Autodiscover service. To troubleshoot, administrators should first verify that the client device has network access to the Exchange server and that firewall rules or proxy configurations are not blocking MAPI over HTTP traffic. Ensuring that the Autodiscover service is properly configured and functioning is equally important, as this service provides the necessary configuration details to MAPI clients during the connection process.

Another common problem is authentication failures when attempting to initiate a MAPI session. These issues often present as repeated credential prompts or outright denial of access. In many cases, the problem stems from inconsistencies between the client's cached credentials and those stored in Active Directory. Clearing cached credentials and ensuring that the user's account is not locked or disabled can resolve this situation. Additionally, administrators should confirm that the client and server are both configured to use compatible authentication methods, such as NTLM or Kerberos, and that any security policies such as conditional access or multi-factor authentication have been properly accounted for in the client configuration.

Outlook clients that rely on MAPI may also encounter performance-related issues, such as slow message retrieval, lag when switching between folders, or delays in sending and receiving emails. These symptoms can be attributed to problems with the MAPI cache, oversized mailboxes, or network latency. In troubleshooting such scenarios, clearing and rebuilding the Outlook Offline Storage Table (OST) file is often an effective solution. Additionally, reviewing mailbox quotas and recommending users to archive old emails or reorganize large folders can improve performance. Administrators should also evaluate the Exchange server's health and capacity, checking for issues such as high disk latency, memory bottlenecks, or overloaded databases that could be impacting MAPI performance for multiple users.

MAPI profile corruption is another issue that frequently disrupts communication workflows. Symptoms may include Outlook crashes, missing folders, or error messages when performing basic tasks like sending an email or opening a calendar item. Profile corruption can be caused by sudden application terminations, failed updates, or inconsistencies between the client and server data. To resolve this issue, creating a new Outlook profile is a standard troubleshooting step. Administrators may automate profile creation using tools such as the Office Deployment Tool or Group Policy settings to streamline this process across multiple devices.

Calendar synchronization problems also surface in MAPI environments, especially in organizations with shared calendars and resource bookings. Users may report missing appointments, duplicate entries, or discrepancies between Outlook and mobile devices. Troubleshooting calendar sync issues involves verifying that free/busy information is correctly published and accessible. Administrators should check the Availability Service on the Exchange server and ensure that public folders or shared mailboxes used for calendar sharing are configured with appropriate permissions. In some cases, inconsistencies may be caused by third-party add-ins or mobile device sync issues, requiring a broader investigation that includes Exchange ActiveSync logs and add-in compatibility checks.

Another challenging MAPI issue is related to public folder access. Users may encounter permission errors or be unable to see certain public folders despite having been granted access. This problem can stem from incorrect folder permissions, replication issues between public folder databases, or corruption within the public folder hierarchy. Troubleshooting involves verifying permissions using tools like Exchange Management Shell or Exchange Admin Center. Administrators may also need to check for replication errors, especially in multi-site deployments, where public folder data must synchronize across different Exchange servers.

MAPI errors may also occur in custom applications that leverage Extended MAPI for automation or integration purposes. Developers often encounter problems such as failed MAPI calls, unexpected NULL pointers, or unhandled exceptions. To troubleshoot these issues, developers should first ensure that their application is using the correct version of the MAPI libraries and that proper error-handling routines are in place. Logging MAPI API calls and examining returned HRESULT codes can provide valuable insights into where and why failures are occurring. It is also important to confirm that the custom application has the necessary permissions to access messaging data, particularly if it operates using service accounts or is designed to run unattended.

Security-related MAPI issues are increasingly common in environments that enforce encryption, digital signatures, or data loss prevention policies. For instance, messages may fail to send if S/MIME certificates are missing, expired, or improperly configured. In such cases, administrators should verify that valid certificates are present in the user's personal certificate store and that they match the user's email address. In organizations where DLP policies are enforced at the transport level, administrators must also review policy configurations to ensure that legitimate messages are not being blocked or quarantined due to overly restrictive rules.

Advanced diagnostic tools are critical in the troubleshooting process for MAPI-related issues. Microsoft provides tools such as MFCMAPI, which allows administrators and developers to directly inspect MAPI objects within a mailbox or message store. MFCMAPI can be used to identify corrupt items, clear problematic properties, and troubleshoot mailbox-level problems. Additionally, network diagnostic tools like Wireshark can capture MAPI over HTTP traffic, allowing administrators to pinpoint connection problems or identify issues related to SSL/TLS handshakes. Exchange-specific diagnostic logs, such as HTTP proxy logs or Autodiscover logs, also play an important role in identifying server-side misconfigurations that may impact MAPI performance or connectivity.

Troubleshooting MAPI issues requires a comprehensive understanding of both the client and server components, as well as the network infrastructure and security controls that govern their interaction. By following a structured approach and utilizing diagnostic tools effectively, administrators and support teams can quickly identify the root causes of common MAPI problems and implement corrective actions. Maintaining robust documentation of recurring issues and resolutions also helps organizations build a knowledge base that accelerates future troubleshooting efforts, ultimately contributing to a more stable and resilient messaging environment.

MAPI and Mobile Integration in Modern Enterprises

In today's fast-paced business world, mobile integration has become a cornerstone of enterprise operations, enabling employees to stay connected and productive from virtually anywhere. As organizations increasingly adopt mobile-first strategies, integrating MAPI, or Messaging Application Programming Interface, with mobile platforms has become critical to bridging traditional messaging systems with the growing need for remote and on-the-go access. MAPI's deep integration with Microsoft Exchange and Outlook allows for a secure, scalable, and reliable communication experience, but extending these capabilities to mobile devices introduces unique challenges and opportunities for modern enterprises.

Historically, MAPI was designed with desktop applications in mind, primarily for Microsoft Outlook running on Windows. The full functionality of MAPI allowed desktop users to access a comprehensive set of messaging features such as emails, calendars, contacts, tasks, public folders, and shared mailboxes. However, as businesses began shifting toward a more mobile workforce, there arose a need to ensure that this same level of access was available on smartphones, tablets, and other portable devices. To meet this demand, Microsoft evolved MAPI to support mobile environments, most notably through the implementation of MAPI over HTTP, which improved reliability, performance, and compatibility with mobile and remote access scenarios.

MAPI over HTTP replaced the older RPC over HTTP transport protocol and was specifically designed to improve the mobile experience. It offers faster connection establishment, better session resilience, and more efficient data handling, making it well-suited for mobile devices that often contend with fluctuating network conditions and intermittent connectivity. Through MAPI over HTTP, mobile applications such as Outlook for iOS and Android can establish secure, persistent connections to Exchange servers, providing users with real-time synchronization of emails, calendars, and contacts, regardless of location.

One of the key advantages of MAPI integration in mobile environments is the seamless synchronization of business-critical data. Mobile users can access up-to-date inboxes, schedule and accept calendar invitations, view shared calendars, and manage tasks from their devices with the same ease and functionality as they would from their desktop Outlook clients. This level of synchronization is vital for ensuring business continuity, especially for traveling executives, sales teams, and field service personnel who rely heavily on their mobile devices to maintain contact with colleagues, customers, and partners while working outside the office.

Security remains one of the most significant considerations when integrating MAPI with mobile platforms. Since mobile devices are more vulnerable to loss, theft, and unsecured networks, MAPI communication is fortified through transport-level encryption using SSL and TLS protocols. This ensures that data in transit between mobile applications and Exchange servers is protected from eavesdropping and tampering. Moreover, enterprises often implement mobile device management (MDM) solutions in conjunction with MAPI-based applications to enforce additional security controls. These controls may include requiring device encryption, enforcing password policies, enabling remote wipe capabilities, and restricting access to only approved devices.

Another critical aspect of MAPI's role in mobile integration is the ability to support offline access and synchronization. In mobile environments, users frequently experience periods without stable internet connectivity. MAPI, through its efficient session management and synchronization processes, enables mobile clients to cache messages, calendar items, and contacts locally. This allows users to continue working offline and automatically sync changes back to the Exchange server once connectivity is restored. This functionality is essential for maintaining productivity during travel or in areas with limited network infrastructure.

The integration of MAPI with mobile applications also allows for the automation of workflows that are initiated on mobile devices. For example, when a sales representative receives a client inquiry via email on their mobile device, MAPI-based synchronization ensures that the message is instantly available across all endpoints, including the organization's CRM system. This seamless flow of information across platforms ensures that business processes are not delayed due to mobile usage. Additionally, calendar invites sent from mobile devices using MAPI are immediately reflected in organizational calendars, enabling real-time scheduling and resource planning across departments.

MAPI also supports enhanced collaboration through its ability to integrate mobile users with shared mailboxes and public folders. For teams that manage shared resources such as support inboxes or project-specific folders, MAPI ensures that mobile users have the same access to these shared environments as their desktop counterparts. This capability is critical for ensuring that distributed teams, including those who are fully remote or mobile, remain connected to shared communication channels, project updates, and customer correspondence.

In addition to standard email and calendar functions, MAPI's mobile integration extends to custom enterprise applications. Many organizations develop proprietary mobile apps that leverage MAPI to automate messaging workflows or integrate with backend systems. For instance, a logistics company might deploy a mobile app for delivery drivers that automatically generates and sends delivery confirmations via MAPI-based emails to clients upon successful deliveries. This type of custom integration streamlines operations and reduces manual reporting, allowing employees in the field to focus on their core tasks.

Enterprises also benefit from MAPI's ability to work alongside other Microsoft services, such as Microsoft Intune and Azure Active Directory, which offer additional layers of identity protection, device compliance, and application management. Together, these services create a secure and integrated ecosystem where MAPI-powered mobile applications can operate under centralized security and compliance policies. This approach ensures that sensitive business data remains protected even when accessed from a variety of mobile devices and geographic locations.

The shift toward hybrid work models and globally distributed teams has further increased the demand for reliable mobile integration of enterprise messaging systems. Employees expect to have access to business-critical communication tools on their smartphones and tablets as readily as they do on their laptops or office desktops. MAPI's ability to deliver a consistent user experience across platforms is instrumental in meeting these expectations. Whether an employee is checking their inbox on their phone while traveling or scheduling a meeting from their tablet in a remote location, MAPI ensures that the experience is uniform, secure, and fully synchronized with the organization's Exchange infrastructure.

MAPI's role in mobile integration is not limited to user-facing applications. It also supports backend processes such as mobile device auditing, compliance enforcement, and reporting. By enabling centralized visibility into mobile messaging activity, IT administrators can monitor usage patterns, enforce security configurations, and generate reports that demonstrate adherence to corporate and regulatory requirements.

The growing reliance on mobile technologies in modern enterprises has made MAPI an indispensable component for delivering secure, real-time access to messaging systems from virtually any device. As businesses continue to invest in mobility solutions to support remote work, field operations, and client engagement, MAPI's ability to integrate seamlessly with mobile platforms ensures that communication remains efficient, secure, and fully aligned with enterprise workflows. Its flexibility and security-first approach make it a key driver of productivity and collaboration in today's mobile-first business landscape.

Enhancing Collaboration with MAPI

Collaboration is the lifeblood of any modern organization, and effective communication tools are crucial in enabling teams to work together efficiently, regardless of geographic location or time zone. MAPI, or Messaging Application Programming Interface, has long been at the center of enterprise communication, serving as the bridge between client applications and Microsoft Exchange, the core messaging platform for many businesses. By facilitating seamless interaction with email, calendars, contacts, tasks, and public folders,

MAPI provides the technical foundation for enhanced collaboration across departments, business units, and global teams.

One of the most significant ways MAPI enhances collaboration is by enabling real-time access to shared resources. Through MAPI's deep integration with Exchange, users can easily access shared mailboxes and public folders from client applications like Microsoft Outlook. Shared mailboxes are commonly used by teams that manage customer service inquiries, project communications, or department-level correspondence. With MAPI, team members can read, respond to, and manage emails within these shared mailboxes as if they were part of their own mailbox. This allows multiple employees to collaborate on incoming requests, coordinate responses, and track progress on open issues, all within a centralized communication hub.

Public folders offer another collaborative benefit, as they allow teams to organize and share not just emails but also documents, contacts, calendars, and notes. MAPI facilitates the creation, modification, and synchronization of public folders across the organization. This enables project teams to maintain dedicated spaces where project-related emails, documents, and meeting notes are easily accessible to all stakeholders. By removing the barriers created by isolated inboxes or departmental silos, MAPI-integrated public folders promote knowledge sharing and ensure that all relevant information is available to those who need it.

Calendar sharing and coordination is another critical area where MAPI enhances collaboration. In large organizations, scheduling meetings and coordinating activities among busy teams can be a logistical challenge. MAPI allows client applications to seamlessly access and manage shared calendars, enabling users to view the availability of colleagues, book meeting rooms, and schedule group events. The integration of MAPI with the Availability Service in Exchange makes it possible for users to instantly check free/busy information, reducing the time spent on back-and-forth communication to find mutually convenient meeting times. Furthermore, MAPI ensures that updates to meeting requests, such as time changes or cancellations, are automatically synchronized across all participants' calendars, eliminating confusion and maintaining alignment.

MAPI also plays a crucial role in supporting delegated access, a feature that is especially useful in executive and administrative workflows. Executives often rely on assistants to manage their schedules, organize meetings, and respond to emails on their behalf. MAPI enables client applications to assign granular permissions that allow designated delegates to act as proxies. Through delegated access, assistants can create calendar events, manage inboxes, and handle correspondence for executives without disrupting the workflow or compromising security. This arrangement fosters a more efficient division of labor and enables senior leaders to focus on strategic priorities while administrative staff manage operational details.

Collaboration is further enhanced through MAPI's integration with task management and workflow automation. Within Outlook, tasks can be assigned, tracked, and updated, providing teams with a simple yet effective way to manage responsibilities and deadlines. MAPI allows developers to integrate these task management capabilities with other business applications, such as project management or CRM systems. For example, when a sales opportunity is created in a CRM platform, a task can be automatically generated and assigned via MAPI to the responsible account manager's Outlook task list. This tight integration ensures that key action items are visible within the user's primary communication and productivity tool, reducing the likelihood of missed deadlines and improving overall accountability.

The notification system provided by MAPI further contributes to dynamic collaboration. MAPI-enabled applications can subscribe to real-time notifications about changes to specific folders, messages, or calendar events. This allows teams to build custom workflows that react instantly to changes within the messaging system. For instance, when a new message is added to a shared mailbox's urgent folder, a notification could be triggered to alert the entire customer support team or escalate the issue to management. These automated alerts help teams respond more quickly to critical developments and reduce the latency between information receipt and action.

MAPI's ability to extend collaboration beyond email and calendar functions is one of its key strengths. By interacting with other elements of the Exchange environment, such as the Global Address List, MAPI enables organizations to integrate directory services into collaborative workflows. Users can easily locate colleagues, departments, or distribution groups based on various attributes such as department, job title, or location. This simplifies internal communication and helps employees identify the right stakeholders when working on cross-functional projects or seeking subject matter expertise.

The flexibility of MAPI also supports the development of custom solutions tailored to specific business needs. Enterprises can build applications that leverage MAPI to automate complex collaboration scenarios. For example, a legal team could develop a document review workflow where contracts submitted via email are automatically routed to the appropriate legal staff for review and feedback. Once comments are incorporated, the application could use MAPI to distribute the revised documents to all involved parties, schedule follow-up meetings, and archive correspondence in a designated public folder for audit purposes.

With the rise of hybrid and remote work models, MAPI plays an essential role in maintaining collaborative continuity across distributed teams. Whether employees are working from headquarters, satellite offices, or home offices, MAPI ensures that their Outlook clients remain fully synchronized with the Exchange server, providing consistent access to shared mailboxes, calendars, and other collaborative tools. By supporting MAPI over HTTP, modern Exchange environments enable secure and efficient remote access, helping organizations maintain high levels of productivity even as employees work from various locations.

Security is an integral part of any collaboration platform, and MAPI is no exception. By leveraging authentication mechanisms integrated with Active Directory, MAPI ensures that only authorized users can access shared resources. Permissions can be customized at the folder or mailbox level, allowing administrators to enforce strict access controls while still enabling collaboration where appropriate. Additionally, MAPI's support for encryption protocols such as SSL/TLS ensures that data remains protected during transmission, safeguarding sensitive communications and collaborative content from interception.

MAPI enhances collaboration by providing the underlying infrastructure that allows teams to communicate, share information, and coordinate actions effectively. Its integration with Microsoft Exchange and Outlook supports a wide array of collaboration scenarios, from shared mailboxes and calendars to automated workflows and real-time notifications. In an increasingly connected and fast-moving business environment, MAPI remains a critical enabler of teamwork and information flow, empowering organizations to operate with agility and cohesion across all levels.

MAPI and Unified Communications Solutions

The modern enterprise landscape is increasingly shaped by the demand for streamlined, efficient communication channels that transcend traditional barriers. Unified Communications, or UC, has emerged as a strategic approach that consolidates various communication tools into a single, integrated platform. MAPI, or Messaging Application Programming Interface, plays a significant role in enabling organizations to bring together email, calendaring, contacts, and task management within the broader context of unified communications solutions. By providing deep integration with Microsoft Exchange and Outlook, MAPI ensures that email and messaging services remain core components of UC environments while seamlessly connecting with voice, video, chat, and collaboration tools.

Unified Communications solutions aim to eliminate the fragmentation caused by disjointed systems, enabling employees to communicate and collaborate more effectively, regardless of the medium or device they are using. MAPI is instrumental in achieving this objective by providing applications with direct access to critical messaging services. In UC ecosystems, where chat, voice, and video meetings are often combined with email-based workflows, MAPI ensures that email remains tightly integrated with other communication channels. For example, when a user schedules a video conference using a UC platform like Microsoft Teams, the underlying MAPI integration with Outlook ensures that the meeting invitation is sent via email and automatically added to attendees' calendars within their Exchange mailboxes.

MAPI's integration into unified communications solutions also enhances the ability to synchronize presence and availability information across platforms. Presence indicators show whether a colleague is available, busy, away, or offline, helping users determine the best way to initiate communication. MAPI contributes to this functionality by making calendar data available to UC clients, allowing them to reflect real-time availability based on scheduled meetings or appointments. For instance, if a user has a meeting blocked in their Outlook calendar, MAPI provides the necessary data for the UC platform to update their presence status to "In a Meeting" automatically, preventing interruptions and encouraging more respectful communication habits.

Another critical aspect of MAPI's role in UC solutions is its facilitation of contact and directory services. By interacting with the Exchange Global Address List (GAL) through MAPI, UC platforms can access a centralized, organization-wide directory of employees, departments, distribution groups, and external contacts. This enables users to initiate emails, instant messages, voice calls, or video conferences directly from their UC client interfaces without needing to search across multiple disconnected systems. The seamless access to accurate and updated contact information reduces friction and enhances productivity by simplifying the process of reaching the right people.

MAPI also serves as the foundation for many workflow automation scenarios within UC environments. For example, organizations often integrate ticketing or customer relationship management (CRM) systems with their UC solutions to streamline communication with customers and internal teams. MAPI enables these business systems to automatically generate email alerts, schedule meetings, or create calendar appointments as part of a larger automated workflow. When a customer support ticket is escalated, MAPI can be used to trigger an email notification to the appropriate support team, automatically schedule a follow-up meeting in their calendars, and update shared task lists. This reduces manual effort and speeds up resolution times while ensuring that all communication flows through a unified and coordinated system.

In addition to email and calendar integration, MAPI plays a supporting role in compliance and governance within unified communications ecosystems. Many industries are subject to strict regulatory frameworks that require secure archiving and monitoring of all communication channels, including email. MAPI enables UC solutions to capture, archive, and audit email communications seamlessly alongside other forms of communication, such as instant messaging or voice recordings. This unified approach to compliance ensures that organizations have a comprehensive view of all interactions and can easily demonstrate adherence to legal and regulatory standards during audits.

Unified Communications platforms increasingly rely on APIs to integrate diverse communication methods. While modern UC platforms often leverage RESTful APIs such as Microsoft Graph for cloud-native services, MAPI remains indispensable in environments that rely on on-premises Exchange servers or hybrid deployments. Many organizations maintain hybrid models, combining Microsoft 365 services with on-premises Exchange to meet specific security, compliance, or operational requirements. In such environments, MAPI ensures that legacy systems and desktop clients maintain full functionality while coexisting with cloud-based UC components.

The role of MAPI in UC solutions also extends to improving user experience and consistency across devices. Employees using desktop Outlook clients benefit from MAPI's advanced capabilities, such as accessing shared mailboxes, managing complex calendar permissions, and interacting with public folders. Simultaneously, UC platforms integrated with MAPI ensure that mobile and web-based clients maintain access to the same messaging data and functionality. This consistency allows employees to switch between devices without losing context or functionality, supporting the flexible and mobile working practices that modern organizations require.

MAPI's compatibility with workflow and collaboration tools further strengthens its contribution to UC strategies. Many organizations integrate MAPI with platforms like SharePoint or Microsoft Teams to facilitate document sharing, co-authoring, and real-time collaboration. For example, an email thread discussing project deliverables may include a link to a shared document library hosted in SharePoint. MAPI ensures that such emails are fully integrated with Outlook and Exchange, while the UC platform allows teams to discuss, edit, and manage documents collaboratively within a single interface. This deep integration reduces information silos and fosters a more connected digital workplace.

Another advantage of MAPI's role in UC environments is its support for real-time notifications and event-driven workflows. UC platforms can leverage MAPI's notification capabilities to trigger instant updates when specific events occur within the messaging system. For instance, when a high-priority email arrives in a monitored shared mailbox, the UC platform can automatically generate a real-time alert via instant messaging or push notification to relevant team members, ensuring immediate attention and response.

Security is also enhanced through MAPI's integration with UC systems. By leveraging Active Directory authentication and Exchange security policies, MAPI ensures that only authorized users can access messaging resources within the UC ecosystem. Furthermore, transport-level encryption provided by MAPI over HTTP protects data in transit, while S/MIME integration allows for message-level encryption and digital signatures when required. This security-first approach is critical in protecting sensitive business communications and maintaining trust within and outside the organization.

As unified communications continue to evolve, MAPI remains a fundamental enabler of interoperability and integration across diverse platforms. Its ability to tie together the critical functions of email, calendaring, task management, and contact directories with modern voice, video, and chat solutions ensures that enterprises can build cohesive and efficient communication ecosystems. Whether supporting hybrid deployments, enabling cross-platform workflows, or ensuring secure and compliant messaging, MAPI plays a key role in helping organizations deliver on the promise of unified communications in the digital workplace.

Customizing MAPI for Industry-Specific Needs

MAPI, or Messaging Application Programming Interface, is often recognized for its role as a universal solution for integrating messaging systems with client applications such as Microsoft Outlook. However, what makes MAPI particularly valuable for enterprises is its flexibility and extensibility, which allow businesses to customize its implementation to meet specific industry requirements. Every sector, from healthcare and finance to manufacturing and legal services, has distinct operational workflows, regulatory obligations, and communication patterns. MAPI's capacity to be adapted and tailored to these unique demands enables organizations to build bespoke solutions that optimize efficiency, ensure compliance, and enhance collaboration across highly specialized business processes.

In the healthcare sector, the protection of sensitive patient information is paramount. Healthcare providers must comply with stringent regulations such as the Health Insurance Portability and Accountability Act (HIPAA), which mandates the secure handling of protected health information (PHI). By customizing MAPI implementations, healthcare organizations can enforce message-level encryption through automated S/MIME integration for all emails containing PHI. In addition to encryption, MAPI allows healthcare IT teams to develop applications that automatically route sensitive communications through secure gateways, enforce retention policies on clinical correspondence, and ensure that emails are automatically archived to meet regulatory auditing requirements. Custom workflows can also be created to link MAPI-based communication directly with electronic health record (EHR) systems, ensuring that patient records are updated in real time when lab results, appointment confirmations, or discharge summaries are sent via email.

Financial institutions also benefit greatly from MAPI's customization capabilities. Banks, investment firms, and insurance companies operate under the oversight of regulatory bodies that demand strict adherence to data retention, security, and reporting guidelines, including SOX, PCI DSS, and GDPR. Custom MAPI solutions in the financial industry often involve integrating MAPI workflows with transaction processing systems or customer relationship management (CRM) platforms to automate communication with clients regarding account statements, investment portfolio updates, and regulatory disclosures. Additionally, MAPI can be configured to tag messages with custom properties that align with internal compliance classifications, such as risk categories, client segmentation, or transaction types. These custom tags can trigger additional workflows, such as escalating high-risk transactions for managerial approval or routing flagged communications through a data loss prevention (DLP) system for further inspection.

Manufacturing and supply chain operations require timely communication across departments and external partners to ensure smooth production and distribution. Customizing MAPI for manufacturing environments often involves automating alert systems that notify stakeholders of production delays, inventory shortages, or shipping updates. For instance, when an ERP system detects that raw materials have not arrived on schedule, MAPI-enabled processes can automatically generate and distribute status reports to procurement managers, logistics coordinators, and key suppliers. Manufacturing firms can also use MAPI to create specialized public folders for collaborative access to quality control documentation, production schedules, or maintenance logs, ensuring that all parties have up-to-date information readily available within their messaging environment.

The legal industry presents another compelling case for MAPI customization. Law firms and legal departments manage vast volumes of sensitive documents and client communications, all of which must be carefully tracked and secured. By customizing MAPI integrations, legal teams can automate the secure transmission of contracts, case files, and court filings. MAPI can also be leveraged to create workflows where emails tagged with certain keywords, such as "confidential" or "privileged," are automatically archived in secure document management systems or routed for partner-level approval before being sent externally. In addition, custom MAPI applications can link case management software with Outlook, enabling attorneys to manage case-related correspondence and deadlines directly from their email client, improving efficiency and reducing the risk of missed court dates or contractual obligations.

In industries such as energy and utilities, MAPI customization supports field operations by facilitating better communication between field technicians and central office staff. Custom mobile applications can be developed using MAPI to automatically generate status reports or incident notifications from remote locations. For example, when a field engineer completes an inspection or repair at a remote site, a MAPI-enabled application can capture the relevant data and automatically send a detailed report, along with photos and GPS coordinates, to supervisors and project managers. This allows decision-makers to access real-time information from the field, improving response times and coordination across dispersed teams.

MAPI's support for custom service providers enables organizations to build entirely new components tailored to their specific industries. For instance, transportation companies can develop a custom MAPI transport provider that integrates with proprietary scheduling or routing platforms. This transport provider could automatically dispatch emails to drivers or terminal managers with updated delivery instructions, route changes, or compliance documents. The flexibility of Extended MAPI allows these service providers to interact seamlessly with both the core messaging infrastructure and external business applications, creating an integrated communication system that directly supports operational objectives.

The education sector also benefits from industry-specific MAPI customizations. Universities and schools can leverage MAPI to integrate student information systems with faculty and administrative messaging tools. Automated notifications regarding exam schedules, class cancellations, or academic performance updates can be generated and distributed to students and parents through MAPI-enabled processes. Additionally, MAPI can be used to manage shared calendars for classroom and facility bookings, ensuring that instructors and administrative staff can coordinate effectively without conflicts. Custom workflows can also be implemented to handle sensitive student data securely, adhering to privacy laws such as FERPA.

Across all industries, MAPI's ability to work in hybrid environments supports the unique operational demands of organizations with both on-premises and cloud-based infrastructure. Companies that have yet to fully migrate to Microsoft 365 or maintain legacy systems for regulatory reasons can still benefit from customized MAPI workflows that integrate with modern collaboration tools, including Microsoft Teams and SharePoint. MAPI customization enables these organizations to bridge communication gaps, automate repetitive tasks, and ensure that critical information is shared efficiently across diverse platforms and departments.

Security remains an overarching concern in every sector, and MAPI customization enables businesses to implement tailored security controls within their messaging workflows. Custom MAPI applications can enforce organization-specific encryption standards, apply digital signatures to sensitive emails, or automatically log message activity for auditing purposes. These security measures can be aligned with sector-specific regulations, giving organizations confidence that their communication processes meet legal and operational standards.

By offering an extensive set of APIs and deep integration capabilities, MAPI provides a flexible platform that organizations can adapt to meet the specialized demands of their industries. Customizing MAPI not only enhances productivity and workflow efficiency but also ensures that communication systems are aligned with the specific compliance, security, and operational challenges unique to each sector. The ability to tailor MAPI implementations allows businesses to leverage messaging infrastructure as a powerful driver of industry-specific innovation and competitive advantage.

MAPI APIs: Extending Business Application Capabilities

MAPI APIs, or Messaging Application Programming Interface APIs, are powerful tools that enable developers to integrate, extend, and automate messaging functionality within business applications. While MAPI is traditionally associated with enabling Microsoft Outlook to communicate with Exchange servers, its underlying APIs offer far greater flexibility, opening up a world of possibilities for organizations looking to enhance their business processes and build custom communication workflows. MAPI APIs provide programmatic access to emails, calendars, contacts, tasks, public folders, and even lower-level system components, allowing businesses to tightly integrate messaging functions with line-of-business applications and automate complex workflows.

At the heart of MAPI APIs is the ability to manipulate the core messaging objects within Microsoft Exchange. This includes direct access to objects such as sessions, message stores, folders, messages, attachments, and address books. By interacting with these objects through the MAPI API, developers can build applications that not only send and receive messages but also perform advanced operations such as categorizing emails, automating responses, generating meeting requests, or integrating with CRM, ERP, and project management systems. For example, a business application could be programmed to automatically create and send customer notifications based on events in a supply chain management system, ensuring that clients are updated in real-time on shipment status or delivery confirmations.

MAPI APIs provide a rich and granular property model that allows developers to read and write a wide array of metadata associated with each messaging object. For instance, when working with a message object, the API allows access to properties such as the subject, sender, recipients, message body, read status, priority flags, and custom user-defined fields. This flexibility makes it possible to enrich business workflows with contextual data extracted directly from communications. Applications can be designed to automatically flag certain messages based on keywords, trigger workflows based on sender or recipient domains, or archive messages in specific folders according to business rules.

One of the most valuable features of MAPI APIs is the ability to create custom service providers. Service providers act as modular components within the MAPI architecture and allow developers to extend the default behavior of the messaging system. For instance, a business might develop a custom transport provider that integrates MAPI with a proprietary messaging system or a legacy enterprise application. Alternatively, organizations could create custom address book providers that integrate MAPI with external databases or directory services, allowing users to search and interact with contact records stored outside of Exchange or Active Directory. This level of extensibility gives businesses full control over how MAPI-enabled applications interact with their broader IT ecosystems.

MAPI APIs also support direct interaction with Exchange public folders and shared mailboxes, making them essential for building collaborative tools within business applications. For example, developers can create applications that automatically distribute incoming emails to specific public folders based on project codes, customer names, or priority levels, streamlining team workflows and improving information accessibility. Similarly, custom solutions can be built to monitor shared mailboxes and automate actions, such as escalating urgent customer service requests, archiving project correspondence, or generating summary reports based on communication patterns within shared folders.

Beyond facilitating collaboration, MAPI APIs empower businesses to automate repetitive tasks that would otherwise require significant manual effort. By writing custom scripts or applications that interact with MAPI objects, organizations can automate routine actions such as sending meeting invitations, generating follow-up reminders, or updating contact records. For instance, a sales automation tool might use MAPI APIs to automatically generate Outlook calendar events and send invitations to both sales representatives and customers when a new deal reaches a specific stage in the CRM system. The same tool could also use MAPI to send thank-you emails and follow-up surveys after client meetings, ensuring consistency and timeliness across customer interactions.

MAPI APIs are also widely used to enforce security and compliance policies within business applications. By programmatically controlling access to messaging objects, developers can build applications that ensure only authorized users can view, modify, or delete sensitive emails and documents. Additionally, MAPI APIs can be used to automatically apply encryption, digital signatures, or retention tags to emails based on their content or classification. For instance, an internal financial application could leverage MAPI APIs to automatically encrypt all messages containing financial reports before sending them to executive stakeholders, while also archiving a copy in a secure location for compliance purposes.

Another area where MAPI APIs excel is in monitoring and event-driven automation. The notification system within MAPI allows applications to subscribe to changes in messaging stores, folders, or individual items. This enables the creation of event-driven applications that can react in real-time to user actions or system events. For example, an application could be configured to listen for new messages in a critical mailbox and automatically parse the content to trigger workflows, such as creating a new task in a project management system or alerting specific teams via SMS or instant messaging platforms. By responding to events as they happen, businesses can improve agility and responsiveness in customer service, operations, and other time-sensitive areas.

The integration of MAPI APIs with other enterprise systems further amplifies their value. Developers often combine MAPI with APIs from ERP systems, CRM platforms, document management solutions, or cloud services such as Microsoft Graph. This multi-system integration allows for the creation of unified business workflows where messaging functions are fully embedded within larger process automation initiatives. For example, a procurement system might leverage MAPI APIs to automatically generate and email purchase orders to vendors while simultaneously updating internal databases, scheduling delivery dates on shared calendars, and notifying the receiving department of expected shipments.

From a deployment perspective, MAPI APIs offer compatibility with both on-premises Exchange servers and hybrid environments that combine on-premises infrastructure with Microsoft 365 services. This versatility allows businesses to leverage MAPI's capabilities regardless of their existing IT architecture. For organizations that are gradually migrating to the cloud, MAPI APIs can continue to serve as a critical integration layer for legacy systems that must coexist with modern, cloud-based applications.

MAPI APIs provide a powerful and versatile foundation for extending the capabilities of business applications far beyond simple email integration. By enabling direct interaction with messaging objects, facilitating event-driven workflows, supporting custom service providers, and ensuring seamless interoperability with enterprise systems, MAPI APIs empower organizations to create tailored solutions that meet their unique operational and compliance needs. The ability to automate complex processes, enforce security policies, and improve collaboration across departments makes MAPI APIs an indispensable tool for businesses seeking to enhance their messaging infrastructure and drive greater value from their enterprise applications.

Building Scalable MAPI Solutions

Creating scalable MAPI solutions is essential for enterprises seeking to support growing communication needs across distributed teams, multiple departments, and hybrid infrastructure environments. As businesses expand, their messaging systems must be able to handle increasing volumes of email traffic, user connections, automated workflows, and integration points with other business applications. MAPI, or Messaging Application Programming Interface, is a powerful framework that allows developers to build custom applications and services that interact directly with messaging servers like Microsoft Exchange. However, scaling these solutions requires careful planning, optimization, and the implementation of best practices to ensure they perform efficiently under growing workloads.

The foundation of a scalable MAPI solution begins with designing an architecture that can accommodate both current and future demand. At the core of MAPI is the client-server model, where client applications initiate sessions and perform actions on message stores, folders, messages, calendars, and other messaging objects. As more users and applications rely on MAPI to automate processes or manage communication tasks, the number of concurrent sessions and transactions can grow significantly. A scalable MAPI solution must be capable of managing these sessions efficiently to prevent bottlenecks, slowdowns, or service disruptions.

To achieve this, developers should design MAPI applications to use session pooling and resource optimization techniques. Instead of creating a new MAPI session for every transaction, applications can maintain a pool of reusable sessions that are allocated as needed. This reduces overhead on the Exchange server and minimizes latency associated with session initialization and teardown. In high-volume environments, session pooling becomes essential to handle spikes in workload, such as during end-of-month financial reporting or major marketing campaigns where automated messaging is heavily used.

Efficient memory and resource management are critical for building scalable MAPI solutions. MAPI applications often interact with large datasets, including message stores with thousands of emails, calendar items, or contact records. Developers must ensure that their applications are designed to retrieve and process data in manageable chunks, avoiding excessive memory usage or resource exhaustion. For example, when reading messages from a folder, applications should implement pagination or batched processing to handle subsets of messages at a time, rather than attempting to load the entire folder into memory.

As enterprises grow, MAPI solutions may need to operate across multiple Exchange servers or hybrid environments combining on-premises and cloud-based infrastructure. Scalable MAPI applications should be designed with multi-server support in mind, enabling them to connect to and manage messaging resources across geographically dispersed or hybrid environments. Load balancing strategies, such as distributing client requests across multiple Exchange servers, help ensure consistent performance even during periods of high demand. In hybrid environments, MAPI applications should be capable of seamlessly switching between on-premises and cloud mailboxes, adapting to evolving infrastructure without service disruption.

Another key element in scaling MAPI solutions is error handling and fault tolerance. As applications process larger volumes of messages and transactions, the likelihood of encountering transient errors, such as network interruptions or temporary service outages, increases. Scalable MAPI solutions must implement robust error-handling mechanisms that can gracefully recover from failures. For example, when encountering a failed MAPI call, the application should automatically retry the operation with backoff logic to prevent overwhelming the server. Logging errors and monitoring performance metrics is essential to identifying trends and preemptively addressing recurring issues that could impact scalability.

Security and compliance must be embedded into the design of scalable MAPI solutions, particularly for enterprises operating in regulated industries. As message volumes increase, so does the amount of sensitive information flowing through the system. Scalable applications should enforce encryption using SSL/TLS for data in transit and support S/MIME for message-level encryption and digital signatures. Additionally, scalable MAPI solutions must include mechanisms to apply data retention, archiving, and auditing policies to ensure that the organization's expanding communication footprint remains compliant with regulatory requirements.

Automation is a significant driver of scalability in MAPI environments. Applications that automate repetitive tasks, such as generating reports, sending notifications, or processing incoming emails, reduce manual workload and improve operational efficiency. However, as automation scales, developers must carefully manage concurrency and processing capacity. For instance, a MAPI application that monitors multiple shared mailboxes for incoming requests should be designed to process messages asynchronously using worker threads or background services to prevent blocking operations. This allows the system to handle a higher throughput of messages without introducing latency for end-users or degrading performance.

Event-driven architecture patterns are particularly effective in building scalable MAPI solutions. By subscribing to notifications through MAPI's built-in event system, applications can react to changes in the messaging environment in real time. For example, when a new message arrives in a monitored mailbox or a calendar event is modified, the application can immediately trigger downstream workflows. Leveraging event-driven patterns reduces the need for continuous polling, which can strain server resources in high-volume environments. Event subscriptions can also be used to selectively monitor critical folders or items, focusing system resources on the most important communication events.

Integration with other enterprise systems plays a crucial role in building scalable MAPI solutions. Many businesses combine MAPI-enabled applications with ERP, CRM, or document management systems to automate business processes. To maintain scalability, developers must implement efficient data exchange mechanisms between MAPI and external systems. Using lightweight, asynchronous messaging patterns such as message queues or webhooks can decouple components and enable horizontal scaling. For instance, an application that generates customer invoices from an ERP system and sends them via email using MAPI can offload invoice generation to a queue-based system, allowing MAPI to focus solely on message creation and dispatch.

Monitoring and performance optimization are essential for maintaining scalability as the system grows. Administrators should deploy monitoring tools that capture real-time metrics on session usage, transaction volumes, processing times, and error rates. Tools like Microsoft Exchange Performance Monitor, MFCMAPI, or custom telemetry dashboards can provide insights into system health and performance trends. Based on these metrics, administrators can proactively adjust server resources, optimize database performance, or fine-tune application configurations to accommodate rising demand.

Finally, scalability in MAPI solutions also depends on adopting modern coding practices and adhering to Microsoft's recommended development guidelines. Developers should regularly update their applications to leverage the latest MAPI libraries, security patches, and Exchange server features. By following best practices such as minimizing unnecessary MAPI calls, avoiding hard-coded configurations, and modularizing application components, organizations can future-proof their MAPI solutions to support sustained growth and evolving business requirements.

By focusing on efficient resource management, fault tolerance, multi-server support, and real-time automation, businesses can build MAPI solutions that scale with the demands of their expanding operations. Scalable MAPI applications become indispensable assets in ensuring that enterprise communication systems remain reliable, secure, and capable of supporting increasingly complex workflows and growing user bases.

Automating Business Processes with MAPI

The pursuit of efficiency and productivity has led many organizations to focus on automating repetitive and time-consuming business processes. MAPI, or Messaging Application Programming Interface, has long been a key enabler in this regard, offering a robust set of tools that allow businesses to automate a wide range of messaging-related tasks within enterprise environments. MAPI's deep integration with Microsoft Exchange and Microsoft Outlook provides developers with direct access to core messaging functions such as email, calendar, task, contact, and public folder management, making it an ideal platform for embedding automation into day-to-day operations.

One of the most common applications of MAPI in business process automation is in the handling of email workflows. Organizations that process large volumes of transactional emails, customer service inquiries, internal notifications, or approvals can leverage MAPI to streamline and automate these operations. For example, an organization may use MAPI to develop an application that monitors specific mailboxes or folders for incoming emails that match certain criteria, such as specific keywords, sender addresses, or subject lines. Once such an email is detected, the system can automatically route it to the appropriate department, forward it to a shared mailbox, escalate it based on priority, or even generate an automated response. This reduces the need for manual intervention, accelerates response times, and ensures that business rules are consistently applied.

Calendar automation is another key area where MAPI provides significant benefits. Many business processes rely on accurate scheduling of meetings, resource bookings, or project timelines. With MAPI, organizations can automate the creation of calendar events based on triggers from other business applications. For instance, when a new project milestone is reached in a project management system, MAPI can be used to automatically create calendar appointments and send meeting invitations to relevant stakeholders. This ensures that teams stay aligned and reduces the administrative overhead associated with manually coordinating schedules. Additionally, MAPI allows applications to manage recurring events, update or cancel existing appointments, and check attendee availability, enabling businesses to automate even the most complex scheduling tasks.

Task management is another domain where MAPI's automation capabilities shine. In organizations that use Microsoft Outlook to manage personal and team tasks, MAPI can be leveraged to create and assign tasks automatically based on business events. For example, in a sales workflow, a CRM system could trigger the creation of follow-up tasks in Outlook when a lead progresses through the sales funnel. These tasks could be assigned to specific sales representatives, complete with due dates, priority levels, and associated notes. Automating task creation in this manner ensures that critical action items are never missed and that accountability is maintained across teams.

MAPI's ability to work with contact and address book data allows organizations to automate customer or partner communication workflows. By integrating MAPI with customer relationship management platforms, businesses can ensure that customer contact details are automatically synchronized with Outlook address books. This integration enables personalized and timely communication, as MAPI-based automation can be used to generate and send messages directly to customer contacts based on updates or events within the CRM system. For example, a financial services firm could use MAPI to automate the distribution of personalized investment reports to clients at the end of each quarter, pulling client data directly from the CRM system and embedding it into customized emails.

Document and file management workflows also benefit greatly from MAPI automation. In industries such as legal services, manufacturing, or finance, where documents such as contracts, invoices, or quality reports must be distributed, MAPI can automate the process of generating and emailing these documents. A document management system could use MAPI to automatically attach the latest version of a contract or report to an email and send it to a predefined list of recipients. By integrating with approval workflows, MAPI can also route documents to reviewers and decision-makers, automatically updating the document's status within the system based on email replies or meeting outcomes.

In addition to automating outbound communication, MAPI is often used to automate inbound workflows by processing incoming messages. Applications can be programmed to parse the content of incoming emails, extract relevant data, and trigger downstream actions within enterprise systems. For example, an application could automatically extract purchase order numbers from vendor emails and feed them into an ERP system for order processing. Similarly, customer service applications can leverage MAPI to automatically create support tickets based on the content of incoming customer inquiries, reducing the time it takes to initiate case resolution.

MAPI's event notification system plays a crucial role in supporting real-time automation. Applications can subscribe to notifications for specific events, such as the arrival of new messages, the creation of calendar appointments, or the modification of contact records. This allows businesses to trigger immediate actions based on real-time changes within the messaging environment. For example, when a high-priority client sends an email to a monitored inbox, a MAPI-enabled system can immediately alert the appropriate account manager via instant message or SMS, ensuring a rapid response to critical communication.

Security and compliance considerations are integrated into automated workflows with MAPI. Businesses can automate the application of security policies, such as ensuring that sensitive emails are encrypted with S/MIME before they are sent, or automatically tagging emails with retention labels based on content classification. For organizations operating in regulated industries, MAPI automation can also enforce compliance rules by archiving specific types of messages in secure storage systems, generating audit logs, and monitoring for policy violations.

Automation through MAPI also improves reporting and analytics within organizations. By programmatically accessing messaging data, businesses can automate the generation of reports that provide insights into communication patterns, response times, and workload distribution. For example, an automated reporting tool could use MAPI to analyze help desk mailbox activity, generating daily reports on ticket volumes, resolution rates, and escalation trends. These insights enable managers to make data-driven decisions and continuously optimize communication workflows.

MAPI's deep integration with Microsoft Exchange ensures that automation solutions built on its framework can scale alongside business growth. Whether automating workflows for a small team or for an enterprise with thousands of employees, MAPI supports high-volume messaging operations, multiple concurrent sessions, and distributed environments that span on-premises and cloud-based infrastructure. This scalability makes MAPI a valuable asset for organizations seeking to modernize their operations and create responsive, automated systems that adapt to changing business needs.

By embedding MAPI into business processes, organizations can eliminate inefficiencies, improve response times, and reduce manual workload across departments. From email and calendar automation to task management, document distribution, and real-time alerts, MAPI serves as a powerful platform for transforming how enterprises manage their communications and operational workflows.

MAPI and Workflow Automation Engines

In today's enterprise landscape, workflow automation engines have become indispensable tools for streamlining business processes, improving efficiency, and ensuring that routine tasks are executed reliably and consistently. When integrated with MAPI, or Messaging Application Programming Interface, these engines gain the ability to interact directly with enterprise messaging systems, unlocking powerful capabilities to automate communication-centric workflows. MAPI acts as the bridge between workflow automation platforms and Microsoft Exchange, providing access to emails, calendars, tasks, contacts, and public folders, while enabling automated solutions to execute messaging tasks that would otherwise require manual intervention.

Workflow automation engines are designed to orchestrate sequences of actions triggered by specific business events. These engines often support drag-and-drop workflow design, enabling IT teams to visually model complex processes such as approval workflows, customer onboarding sequences, document routing, or incident management chains. By incorporating MAPI into these workflows, businesses can automate critical messaging functions as part of broader operational tasks. For instance, in an approval workflow, once a document is submitted for review through a document management system, the workflow engine can leverage MAPI to automatically send an email to the designated approvers, complete with the document attached, a deadline for action, and direct links to approval interfaces.

One of the most common integrations between MAPI and workflow automation engines is the automation of notification processes. Organizations rely heavily on email notifications to alert employees about system events, status updates, compliance warnings, or customer inquiries. By embedding MAPI within the workflow engine, these notifications can be generated automatically, populated with dynamic content, and sent to distribution lists or individual recipients based on the logic defined within the workflow. For example, in a human resources onboarding process, a workflow automation engine could use MAPI to generate personalized welcome emails for new hires, inform IT teams about hardware provisioning tasks, and notify managers about pending onboarding activities, all triggered by the submission of a single onboarding form.

MAPI enhances the functionality of workflow automation engines by providing access to calendar-related actions. Many business workflows are time-sensitive and require the scheduling of meetings, interviews, training sessions, or project deadlines. MAPI integration enables automation engines to create and manage calendar appointments within users' Outlook clients directly. For instance, in a recruitment workflow, after a candidate passes a preliminary interview, the workflow engine can automatically schedule follow-up interviews by generating Outlook calendar invitations for hiring managers and the candidate, taking into account free/busy information to avoid scheduling conflicts. This automation reduces manual coordination efforts and ensures that all stakeholders are aligned on scheduling.

Another key advantage of integrating MAPI with workflow automation engines is the ability to automate email routing and categorization. In large organizations, support tickets, client inquiries, or internal requests are often sent to shared mailboxes or departmental inboxes. With MAPI, automation engines can monitor these mailboxes, analyze incoming emails based on content or metadata, and automatically route them to the appropriate team or folder. For example, a customer service workflow might automatically assign incoming emails to customer support agents based on the region or product mentioned in the message. The system can also prioritize high-urgency emails by flagging them in Outlook and sending escalation notifications to team leads.

MAPI's integration with address books and contact directories further empowers workflow automation. Automation engines can dynamically resolve recipient email addresses based on user roles, departments, or project affiliations by querying the Exchange Global Address List through MAPI. This allows workflows to remain dynamic and adaptable to organizational changes, such as employee onboarding or departmental restructuring. For instance, an IT service request workflow could automatically identify and notify the appropriate technician responsible for a specific office location or business unit without hardcoding individual email addresses into the workflow logic.

MAPI also supports automation engines in managing and auditing communication-based workflows to meet compliance and security requirements. For organizations in regulated industries, such as finance or healthcare, it is critical that all automated messaging processes adhere to data protection standards and are fully auditable. MAPI enables workflow engines to apply encryption to outgoing emails, enforce retention policies by archiving emails into specific folders or secure storage systems, and log all message activity for auditing purposes. This ensures that automated workflows not only improve efficiency but also align with internal policies and external regulatory requirements.

Beyond traditional email workflows, MAPI allows workflow automation engines to facilitate collaborative processes by integrating with shared resources like public folders and shared mailboxes. A procurement approval workflow, for instance, could automatically move approved purchase orders into a public folder accessible by the finance and accounting teams, while rejected orders could be flagged and archived in a separate folder for audit purposes. By automating the movement and organization of documents and messages within the messaging system, organizations can reduce administrative overhead and improve the traceability of critical business processes.

The event-driven capabilities provided by MAPI further extend the value of workflow automation engines. Applications can subscribe to notifications triggered by specific events within the Exchange environment, such as the arrival of new emails, the creation of calendar events, or the modification of contact records. Workflow engines can leverage these real-time triggers to initiate or progress workflows automatically. For example, a facilities management workflow might be configured to monitor a shared mailbox for incoming maintenance requests. When a new request is detected, MAPI can trigger the creation of a maintenance ticket, notify the appropriate technician, and schedule follow-up inspections via Outlook calendar invites.

Integration with MAPI also allows workflow automation engines to streamline document management processes. Many organizations require that documents such as contracts, reports, or compliance forms follow strict approval and distribution workflows. By connecting document management systems with MAPI-enabled workflows, businesses can automatically route documents via email to stakeholders for review, track version history, and generate audit logs to document approval milestones. This eliminates the need for manual document routing and ensures that all communication related to document handling is captured within the messaging system.

As workflow automation engines continue to evolve and support more complex orchestration scenarios, MAPI remains a vital component in extending these capabilities to enterprise messaging platforms. Its ability to provide direct access to core Exchange services enables businesses to build integrated workflows that automate not only backend operations but also front-end communication tasks that drive business processes forward.

By embedding MAPI within workflow automation engines, organizations can unlock new levels of efficiency, consistency, and scalability across departments. The seamless connection between messaging systems and process automation frameworks ensures that communication-dependent workflows operate without delays or human error, supporting faster decision-making and smoother operational execution across the enterprise. MAPI, as a foundational technology, enables automation engines to close the gap between business logic and enterprise communication, empowering organizations to modernize and optimize their business processes.

Cloud-Based MAPI Solutions for Business

The growing shift towards cloud computing has fundamentally changed the way businesses deploy and manage their messaging infrastructures. As organizations transition from traditional on-premises Exchange servers to cloud-based environments such as Microsoft 365, the role of MAPI, or Messaging Application Programming Interface, has evolved to support modern communication needs in a flexible and scalable way. Cloud-based MAPI solutions combine the powerful messaging capabilities of MAPI with the benefits of cloud infrastructure, including reduced overhead, enhanced availability, and seamless integration with distributed teams and applications.

Cloud-based MAPI solutions are designed to work within hybrid and fully cloud-hosted environments. In the past, MAPI was primarily deployed within on-premises Exchange servers, where it facilitated direct communication between Outlook clients and local Exchange infrastructure. With the introduction of Microsoft Exchange Online, MAPI over HTTP was extended to support cloud-hosted mailboxes, enabling client applications and automated systems to interact with cloud-based message stores. This development has allowed businesses to maintain the same deep integration with messaging services while leveraging the scalability and resilience of the cloud.

One of the key advantages of cloud-based MAPI solutions is their ability to simplify infrastructure management. By moving mailboxes and related services to Microsoft 365, organizations eliminate the need to maintain complex on-premises Exchange servers, backup systems, and disaster recovery solutions. Cloud service providers assume responsibility for server maintenance, patching, high availability configurations, and data redundancy. This enables IT teams to focus on strategic initiatives rather than day-to-day maintenance tasks, while still leveraging MAPI-based integrations to automate and enhance communication workflows across the business.

Scalability is another major benefit of cloud-based MAPI solutions. As organizations grow and expand their operations globally, cloud infrastructure ensures that messaging services can scale elastically to meet increasing demands. Whether adding new users, expanding to additional regions, or integrating new applications with Exchange Online, MAPI solutions hosted in the cloud can adapt quickly to changing business needs. The ability to dynamically scale up or down without significant capital expenditure is a critical advantage for businesses that experience seasonal fluctuations or rapid growth.

Cloud-based MAPI solutions also enhance mobility and remote work capabilities. With MAPI over HTTP enabling secure connections from anywhere, employees can access their mailboxes, shared calendars, and other Exchange resources via Outlook and other MAPI-enabled applications without being tied to corporate networks. Remote workers, mobile employees, and distributed teams benefit from consistent access to messaging services, while administrators maintain full control over security policies and user permissions through Microsoft 365's centralized management tools.

Security is a top priority when deploying MAPI solutions in the cloud. Microsoft 365 and Exchange Online integrate robust security features such as data encryption in transit and at rest, multi-factor authentication, conditional access policies, and advanced threat protection. MAPI sessions initiated by client applications or automated workflows leverage these built-in security protocols to protect sensitive communications. Additionally, businesses can implement message-level security using S/MIME or Rights Management Services (RMS) to ensure that critical emails and attachments are encrypted and accessible only to authorized recipients.

Integration with cloud-based MAPI also facilitates seamless hybrid deployments, where businesses maintain some Exchange services on-premises while moving others to the cloud. This hybrid approach is common among organizations that have specific regulatory or operational reasons to retain certain workloads locally. MAPI enables smooth coexistence between on-premises and cloud-hosted mailboxes, allowing users to interact with both environments as if they were part of a single unified messaging infrastructure. Hybrid deployments leverage MAPI over HTTP to provide consistent access to mailboxes, public folders, and shared calendars regardless of where the resources are physically located.

Cloud-based MAPI solutions also play a vital role in supporting application-level integrations. Many enterprises rely on MAPI to enable business-critical applications such as customer relationship management platforms, enterprise resource planning systems, or workflow automation engines to interact directly with messaging services. In the cloud, these applications can use MAPI-enabled services to generate and send transactional emails, automate notifications, or manage meeting requests in Exchange Online mailboxes. This direct integration streamlines business processes, improves information flow, and reduces manual workload across departments.

Automation of business workflows is further enhanced by the availability of MAPI capabilities within cloud-hosted environments. Applications running in cloud platforms like Microsoft Azure or third-party environments can leverage MAPI to create automated processes for handling customer inquiries, sending reports, managing compliance alerts, or routing emails based on content analysis. For example, a cloud-hosted CRM application could use MAPI to automatically generate and send onboarding emails to new customers, complete with calendar invitations for introductory calls, links to knowledge base articles, and personalized account information.

Another benefit of cloud-based MAPI is its ability to facilitate disaster recovery and business continuity. With Exchange Online hosted in Microsoft's global data centers, businesses benefit from built-in redundancy, geo-replication, and automated failover capabilities. In the event of a regional outage or data center failure, mailboxes remain accessible, and MAPI-based applications can continue to operate with minimal disruption. This level of resilience is difficult to achieve with on-premises infrastructure alone and is a key factor driving many organizations toward cloud adoption.

Analytics and reporting capabilities are also enhanced through cloud-based MAPI solutions. Microsoft 365 provides administrators with comprehensive dashboards and reporting tools that offer insights into email traffic patterns, usage trends, compliance status, and security events. MAPI-based applications can also integrate with these reporting tools to generate custom reports on automated messaging workflows, communication volumes, or performance metrics. This data helps businesses make informed decisions about optimizing communication processes and ensuring that automated solutions continue to deliver value as the organization evolves.

The flexibility of cloud-based MAPI solutions allows them to support a wide variety of use cases across industries. In healthcare, MAPI integrations can automate patient appointment reminders and streamline communication between care teams. In financial services, MAPI-enabled applications can automate transaction notifications, customer updates, and compliance communications. In manufacturing, MAPI-based workflows can manage supplier updates, production schedules, and logistics coordination. The cloud ensures that these solutions are accessible, secure, and capable of supporting business operations at scale.

By combining the robust messaging capabilities of MAPI with the scalability, security, and resilience of cloud infrastructure, organizations can create modern, efficient communication ecosystems that adapt to evolving business needs. Cloud-based MAPI solutions enable businesses to automate critical workflows, enhance collaboration, and ensure consistent access to messaging services across global teams. As cloud adoption continues to grow, MAPI remains a key enabler of enterprise messaging, supporting digital transformation initiatives and delivering measurable business value.

MAPI in Hybrid and Multi-Cloud Environments

The evolution of enterprise IT infrastructure has shifted from traditional on-premises systems to more complex hybrid and multi-cloud environments. Businesses now leverage a mix of private data centers, public cloud services, and hosted applications to meet their operational and strategic needs. In this landscape, MAPI, or Messaging Application Programming Interface, continues to play a critical role by providing robust messaging functionality across diverse deployment models. As organizations strive to maintain seamless communication between on-premises Exchange servers and cloud-based services such as Microsoft 365 or other cloud providers, MAPI offers a bridge that connects these environments, enabling a unified messaging experience for users and automated systems alike.

In a hybrid environment, businesses maintain part of their messaging infrastructure on-premises while migrating selected workloads to the cloud. This approach is common among enterprises that need to comply with regulatory requirements, manage legacy systems, or retain control over specific data repositories. MAPI over HTTP is at the heart of hybrid messaging solutions, facilitating secure and efficient communication between client applications and mailboxes, regardless of whether those mailboxes are hosted on an on-premises Exchange server or in Exchange Online. This seamless access is essential for organizations seeking to provide a consistent user experience across hybrid environments, where users expect Outlook or other MAPI-enabled applications to function identically regardless of mailbox location.

One of the key benefits of MAPI in hybrid deployments is its ability to support coexistence. During the migration process, enterprises often operate with a mixed environment where some mailboxes reside in the cloud and others remain on-premises. MAPI enables client applications to communicate with both systems without requiring users to switch between interfaces or change their workflows. A user working with an Outlook client connected to an on-premises Exchange mailbox can still schedule meetings with colleagues using Exchange Online, access shared calendars, and manage tasks as if all resources were hosted in a single environment. MAPI ensures that these interactions are transparent and efficient, enabling businesses to transition to the cloud at their own pace.

MAPI's role in multi-cloud environments is equally significant. While Microsoft Exchange Online is the most common cloud-hosted messaging platform, many enterprises integrate MAPI-enabled applications with additional cloud services, such as Amazon Web Services (AWS), Google Cloud Platform (GCP), or private cloud providers. In multi-cloud architectures, organizations often leverage best-of-breed solutions from different vendors, combining Exchange Online with cloud-based file storage, workflow automation engines, or customer relationship management systems. MAPI acts as a unifying protocol that allows applications running in these diverse environments to access messaging functionality such as sending emails, creating calendar events, or automating task assignments through Exchange servers hosted either on-premises or in the Microsoft cloud.

MAPI is essential for enabling automated workflows that span hybrid and multi-cloud environments. For example, a business might operate a financial application on a private cloud infrastructure while using Exchange Online for messaging and Microsoft Teams for collaboration. Through MAPI integration, the financial application can automate the generation and delivery of financial statements to clients via secure email, update shared calendars with payment reminders, or trigger notifications for approval workflows, all while interacting with Exchange services that exist in the public cloud. This integration ensures that critical business processes remain efficient and coordinated, even as they draw from resources located across multiple environments.

Security and compliance are key considerations when deploying MAPI in hybrid and multi-cloud setups. MAPI communications are secured using protocols such as SSL/TLS, ensuring that data in transit remains encrypted and protected from interception. Furthermore, MAPI-enabled applications in these environments can leverage additional security measures such as Azure Active Directory conditional access policies, multi-factor authentication, and role-based access controls. Organizations operating in regulated industries can enforce data residency and compliance policies by controlling where sensitive data is stored and how it is accessed through MAPI workflows, ensuring adherence to frameworks like GDPR, HIPAA, and industry-specific regulatory guidelines.

One of the technical challenges in hybrid and multi-cloud environments is managing network latency and performance optimization. MAPI over HTTP was specifically designed to address performance concerns in distributed environments, offering faster connection establishment, improved resiliency, and better session management compared to older protocols like RPC over HTTP. This optimization is critical when users and applications need to connect to Exchange services hosted in remote data centers or in the public cloud. By reducing connection overhead and supporting efficient data retrieval and synchronization, MAPI over HTTP helps maintain optimal performance for users and automated processes, even when operating across vast geographic distances.

MAPI also plays a vital role in facilitating interoperability between legacy on-premises systems and modern cloud-based applications. Many enterprises still rely on older ERP, CRM, or document management platforms that were built to interact with on-premises Exchange environments through MAPI. Rather than rewriting these legacy applications to support modern APIs, organizations can maintain compatibility by using MAPI to bridge communication between on-premises systems and cloud-hosted mailboxes. Middleware solutions or custom integration layers can be developed using MAPI to relay messages, synchronize calendar items, or manage contact lists across hybrid or multi-cloud infrastructures, allowing businesses to maximize the value of their existing investments while embracing cloud technologies.

Another significant benefit of MAPI in hybrid and multi-cloud environments is supporting business continuity and disaster recovery strategies. With mailboxes and applications distributed across multiple data centers and cloud regions, MAPI provides the flexibility to redirect traffic and maintain access to messaging services in the event of localized outages or service disruptions. For example, if an on-premises Exchange server experiences downtime, MAPI-enabled applications can be reconfigured to connect to cloud-hosted mailboxes in Exchange Online, ensuring that automated workflows and communication processes continue without interruption.

MAPI's event notification capabilities further enhance workflow automation in hybrid and multi-cloud environments. Applications can subscribe to events within both on-premises and cloud-hosted Exchange environments, enabling real-time reactions to communication events such as new message arrivals, calendar updates, or changes to public folders. This event-driven architecture allows businesses to build integrated workflows that span multiple environments, such as automatically triggering document routing processes or generating compliance reports when specific messaging events occur.

As enterprises increasingly adopt hybrid and multi-cloud strategies, the demand for consistent, scalable, and secure communication workflows grows. MAPI remains a critical enabler of this consistency, allowing businesses to integrate messaging functionality directly into line-of-business applications, workflow automation engines, and collaboration platforms operating across diverse infrastructures. Whether automating approval workflows, streamlining customer communication, or managing project timelines, MAPI provides the foundation needed to ensure that business processes remain synchronized and operational across all layers of the enterprise architecture.

By supporting seamless coexistence, enabling multi-cloud integrations, and ensuring compliance with security and regulatory requirements, MAPI helps organizations unlock the full potential of hybrid and multi-cloud environments. Businesses can confidently expand their operations, migrate workloads, and modernize their messaging infrastructure without sacrificing the depth of integration or the user experience that MAPI has traditionally provided within enterprise communication ecosystems.

The Impact of MAPI on Remote Work

The rapid rise of remote work has transformed how businesses operate and how employees engage with corporate systems and communication tools. Central to the success of remote work is the ability to maintain seamless, secure, and reliable access to enterprise messaging systems from any location. MAPI, or Messaging Application Programming Interface, has played a pivotal role in enabling organizations to adapt to this new model of work by supporting critical communication workflows across distributed teams. Through its integration with Microsoft Exchange and Outlook, MAPI provides employees with full access to email, calendar, contact, and task data, all of which are essential for maintaining productivity and collaboration in a remote work environment.

The transition to remote work necessitated that messaging and collaboration systems function smoothly outside the traditional office network. With MAPI over HTTP, employees are able to establish secure connections to Exchange servers without relying on legacy VPN connections or outdated remote access methods. MAPI over HTTP leverages modern web protocols and encryption standards such as SSL and TLS, enabling Outlook clients and custom MAPI-based applications to securely access mailbox data over the internet. This has allowed businesses to provide their employees with secure remote access to corporate email systems, shared calendars, and public folders, even when working from home, in coworking spaces, or while traveling.

MAPI has ensured that employees working remotely experience the same level of functionality as they would within an office environment. By maintaining direct integration with Exchange servers, MAPI allows users to send and receive emails, manage complex calendar scheduling, create tasks, and access contact lists without any reduction in features. Remote workers are able to book meetings, check colleague availability, respond to shared tasks, and collaborate on projects using shared mailboxes or public folders, all through their familiar Outlook interface or other MAPI-enabled applications. This consistent user experience has been critical in minimizing the disruption associated with transitioning to remote work.

Beyond providing remote access to messaging systems, MAPI has also facilitated the automation of workflows that are essential for supporting distributed teams. Many organizations have leveraged MAPI to automate critical communication processes that ensure remote workers receive timely information and support. For example, human resources departments can automate onboarding workflows that send welcome emails, training schedules, and resource links to new hires working remotely. Similarly, IT teams can automate system status alerts and policy updates by using MAPI to generate and distribute emails to targeted user groups. These automated processes reduce the need for manual coordination and help keep remote employees informed and engaged.

MAPI's impact on remote work also extends to its integration with calendar and scheduling functions. Coordinating meetings across time zones and remote locations is a common challenge for distributed teams. MAPI enables employees to access and manage shared calendars, book conference calls, and schedule virtual meetings with real-time free/busy information, eliminating scheduling conflicts and simplifying coordination. Automated scheduling processes powered by MAPI ensure that invitations to virtual meetings are sent with links to video conferencing platforms, pre-filled agendas, and reminders, streamlining the setup of remote collaboration sessions.

The rise of remote work has increased the demand for secure communication. MAPI supports organizations in enforcing security protocols, such as requiring encryption for sensitive messages and applying digital signatures through S/MIME. For businesses that handle confidential information, including financial records, legal documents, or healthcare data, MAPI's ability to integrate with Exchange's security features has been invaluable in safeguarding sensitive communications in remote settings. By combining secure transport protocols with message-level encryption, organizations can ensure that remote workers are able to communicate securely while remaining compliant with regulatory requirements such as GDPR, HIPAA, or SOX.

MAPI has also played a key role in maintaining business continuity and resilience during unexpected events that force employees to work remotely. During global disruptions, such as the COVID-19 pandemic, organizations with MAPI-enabled messaging systems were able to quickly shift their operations to remote models without compromising productivity. MAPI allowed businesses to maintain critical workflows, such as automated notifications for crisis management, communication of health and safety protocols, and continuity of operations planning. The ability to manage these processes remotely and in real time has contributed to keeping organizations agile and responsive to rapidly changing circumstances.

Additionally, MAPI has supported the seamless integration of third-party applications that are essential for remote work. Many businesses rely on CRM platforms, project management tools, or customer support systems that are integrated with their messaging infrastructure via MAPI. For remote employees, this means that communication-based workflows such as automated customer notifications, support ticket updates, or project task reminders continue to operate smoothly. These integrations ensure that employees are not only connected to their colleagues but also to the business systems that are critical to their roles, regardless of their location.

MAPI's event-driven capabilities have further enhanced its impact on remote work by enabling real-time automation. Remote teams benefit from applications that listen for changes within the Exchange environment and trigger workflows based on specific events. For instance, a remote service desk team might rely on an automated system that monitors a shared mailbox for new support requests and instantly creates tickets, assigns tasks, and sends notifications to the appropriate technician's inbox. Such automation ensures that distributed teams remain responsive and that service-level agreements are maintained, even when employees are working from various locations around the world.

In addition to supporting employee workflows, MAPI has also helped IT administrators manage remote messaging environments more efficiently. Through automated MAPI-based scripts and tools, administrators can remotely configure Outlook profiles, manage mailbox permissions, deploy security policies, and monitor system health. This remote administration capability has been essential in supporting a remote workforce, enabling IT teams to troubleshoot issues, provision accounts, and enforce compliance without requiring physical access to corporate offices or user devices.

As remote work continues to evolve, MAPI remains a critical component in enabling businesses to maintain secure, efficient, and collaborative communication systems. Its ability to support remote access, automate workflows, enhance security, and integrate with business-critical applications has made it a foundational technology for organizations embracing flexible work models. MAPI ensures that employees, regardless of their physical location, have reliable access to the tools and information they need to stay connected, productive, and aligned with organizational goals.

MAPI and Microsoft Exchange Server Integration

The integration of MAPI, or Messaging Application Programming Interface, with Microsoft Exchange Server has long been the backbone of enterprise messaging environments. MAPI provides a powerful and flexible programming interface that allows client applications, such as Microsoft Outlook, as well as custom business applications, to directly interact with the Exchange server's messaging system. This interaction is not limited to basic email operations but extends to a broad range of messaging functions, including access to calendars, contacts, tasks, public folders, and message stores. The deep integration of MAPI with Microsoft Exchange Server has enabled organizations to build scalable, reliable, and feature-rich communication solutions that enhance productivity, automate workflows, and streamline collaboration across departments and teams.

At its core, MAPI facilitates the client-server relationship between applications and Exchange Server by providing an abstraction layer over the transport and data storage mechanisms within the messaging environment. When a MAPI client connects to Exchange, it initiates a session that allows it to access a user's mailbox, manipulate messaging objects, and perform actions such as sending and receiving emails, organizing folders, creating appointments, and managing task lists. This session management is optimized for performance and reliability, ensuring that users experience real-time synchronization between their Outlook client and the Exchange server, regardless of the size of their mailbox or the complexity of their folder structures.

One of the distinguishing features of MAPI and Exchange Server integration is the ability to work with message stores at a granular level. MAPI exposes detailed control over message properties, allowing developers and administrators to manipulate everything from message headers and body content to metadata such as read/unread status, importance flags, and custom properties. This level of control enables organizations to automate business workflows, enforce corporate policies, and integrate Exchange messaging directly into mission-critical applications. For example, a legal department might build a MAPI-based application to automatically categorize and archive emails containing legal contracts into secure public folders, applying metadata tags that support later auditing or eDiscovery processes.

MAPI also serves as the mechanism through which Exchange manages public folders and shared mailboxes. Public folders are collaborative spaces used to store and share emails, documents, and calendar entries among teams and departments. Through MAPI, client applications can create, update, and manage public folders, as well as control user permissions, folder hierarchies, and synchronization rules. This functionality is critical in large organizations where multiple teams rely on shared resources to coordinate project activities, manage group correspondence, or store reference materials. MAPI's ability to provide real-time access to public folders ensures that all users remain aligned and that shared data is available instantly across the enterprise.

The deep integration of MAPI with Exchange Server also supports advanced calendaring and scheduling functionality. MAPI enables Outlook and other client applications to access and manipulate calendar items within Exchange mailboxes, allowing users to create and modify appointments, schedule meetings, and view shared calendars. Furthermore, MAPI interacts with the Exchange Availability Service, enabling users to check free/busy information for colleagues and book meetings based on real-time availability. Businesses rely on this integration to automate scheduling processes, reduce administrative overhead, and ensure that meeting coordination is efficient and free of conflicts.

Security is a foundational component of the MAPI and Exchange Server integration. MAPI sessions authenticate users through Active Directory, providing seamless single sign-on capabilities across enterprise environments. Role-based access controls, configured within Exchange and enforced by MAPI, ensure that users and applications can only access the messaging data they are authorized to manage. MAPI also works in conjunction with Exchange transport rules, encryption policies, and compliance settings to enforce data protection protocols, including message encryption with S/MIME, digital signatures, and automated message journaling.

MAPI's support for event-driven architecture further enhances its integration with Exchange. Applications can subscribe to notifications for specific messaging events, such as the arrival of new messages, updates to calendar events, or changes to folders and contacts. This allows businesses to build automated workflows that respond in real-time to events within the messaging system. For example, a customer support system could leverage MAPI to detect when a new inquiry arrives in a shared support mailbox, automatically create a service ticket, and notify the appropriate agent via email or instant message.

The extensibility of MAPI within Exchange Server allows organizations to integrate messaging functionality with a wide variety of business applications. MAPI can be used to connect Exchange to CRM systems, ERP platforms, document management tools, and workflow automation engines. For instance, sales automation tools might use MAPI to automatically log outbound emails to clients in the CRM system, while project management applications could automate the scheduling of recurring team meetings by directly interfacing with Exchange calendars.

As organizations increasingly adopt hybrid and cloud-first strategies, MAPI continues to serve as a key integration point between on-premises Exchange servers and Exchange Online in Microsoft 365 environments. MAPI over HTTP ensures that client applications and custom-built solutions can interact with mailboxes hosted both locally and in the cloud, supporting seamless coexistence during and after migration projects. This interoperability allows businesses to maintain operational continuity while gradually transitioning to modern cloud infrastructure.

Additionally, MAPI plays a critical role in supporting administrative tasks and user provisioning workflows within Exchange environments. IT administrators frequently use MAPI-enabled scripts and management tools to automate processes such as configuring Outlook profiles, applying mailbox permissions, generating reports on mailbox usage, and performing bulk operations on messaging objects. This automation reduces manual effort, increases efficiency, and ensures consistent implementation of corporate policies across large user populations.

MAPI's close relationship with Exchange Server has contributed significantly to the platform's reputation as one of the most robust and enterprise-ready messaging solutions available. By providing a powerful set of APIs that expose the full range of Exchange functionality, MAPI enables businesses to build tailored solutions that meet their specific communication and collaboration needs. Whether automating the distribution of business-critical reports, integrating with customer service workflows, or ensuring regulatory compliance through secure messaging, MAPI serves as the foundation for achieving operational excellence within Microsoft Exchange environments.

Through its ability to deliver seamless client-server communication, automate workflows, and integrate with line-of-business applications, MAPI continues to be a cornerstone of enterprise messaging infrastructure. Its deep and versatile integration with Microsoft Exchange Server ensures that organizations can adapt their communication strategies to meet the evolving demands of modern business while maintaining security, reliability, and scalability.

MAPI with Outlook: Beyond the Basics

MAPI with Outlook extends far beyond simple email sending and receiving. While many users are familiar with Outlook as a tool for managing emails, calendars, contacts, and tasks, the underlying MAPI technology unlocks advanced capabilities that power a wide variety of business processes and custom applications. MAPI, or Messaging Application Programming Interface, serves as the engine behind Outlook's integration with Microsoft Exchange and other messaging systems. It provides a comprehensive set of APIs that allow developers and administrators to build sophisticated workflows, enhance productivity, and automate communication processes within Outlook.

One of the advanced capabilities that MAPI brings to Outlook is the ability to automate complex email workflows. Businesses that rely on Outlook for customer communications, internal project coordination, or vendor interactions can use MAPI to create customized solutions that manage high-volume email traffic with minimal manual intervention. For instance, customer service departments can leverage

MAPI to automatically monitor specific folders in Outlook and route customer inquiries to the correct support teams based on predefined rules. MAPI can also be used to generate automatic acknowledgment emails, categorize messages, and flag important communications for immediate attention, ensuring a more streamlined and efficient response process.

Beyond automation, MAPI empowers organizations to customize Outlook's user interface and functionality to meet unique business needs. Through MAPI, developers can create custom Outlook forms and ribbon extensions that enhance the way users interact with their inboxes and calendars. For example, a legal team might require a custom email form that includes fields for selecting a case number, tagging a message with a confidentiality level, or attaching billing codes directly from within Outlook. These tailored forms reduce manual data entry and integrate smoothly with backend systems, such as document management platforms or case management databases, thanks to MAPI's ability to facilitate seamless data exchange.

Another area where MAPI extends Outlook's capabilities is in calendaring and scheduling automation. MAPI allows developers to programmatically create, update, and manage Outlook calendar events based on external triggers or business logic. For example, a project management system integrated with Outlook via MAPI can automatically schedule recurring project review meetings, assign them to the relevant teams, and update the agenda when project milestones shift. Furthermore, MAPI provides access to free/busy information within Outlook, allowing custom applications to check participant availability before scheduling meetings. This capability eliminates the inefficiencies caused by scheduling conflicts and helps optimize meeting coordination across teams.

MAPI's deep integration with Outlook also supports contact management beyond the basics. Organizations that manage large contact databases, such as sales teams or event planners, can automate the synchronization of external contact lists with Outlook's address book using MAPI. Contact records from CRM systems or membership databases can be programmatically imported, updated, or organized into custom categories within Outlook. This ensures that users always have access to the most up-to-date contact information without the need for manual import and export procedures. Additionally, MAPI can be used to create dynamic distribution lists based on attributes such as department, client type, or geographic region, further simplifying group communications.

Public folders and shared mailboxes are another feature of Outlook where MAPI adds advanced functionality. MAPI allows custom applications to interact directly with public folders, managing permissions, creating nested folder structures, and automating the movement of messages and documents. For example, an HR department could use a MAPI-based application to organize resumes and applicant correspondence into public folders automatically based on job titles or application stages. Similarly, a finance team could automate the archiving of monthly reports into shared mailboxes or folders accessible by senior management. This structured organization of content within Outlook facilitates better collaboration and ensures that important documents are easily retrievable by authorized users.

MAPI also enables the development of Outlook add-ins that integrate external data and functionality directly into the Outlook interface. For instance, a customer support team might benefit from an add-in that displays ticket information from a helpdesk system alongside incoming customer emails. By leveraging MAPI, such add-ins can access email metadata, message bodies, and attachments to automatically retrieve relevant customer records from external databases. This empowers users to act on emails more effectively without switching between multiple applications.

One of the more advanced uses of MAPI with Outlook is the automation of approval workflows. Many organizations rely on email-based approval chains for processes such as expense reports, project proposals, or contract sign-offs. MAPI enables developers to build automated workflows where approval requests are generated and sent directly from business applications into Outlook. When a user receives an approval email, they can respond directly within Outlook using custom action buttons or forms designed with MAPI. Once a decision is made, the application can automatically log the approval, trigger follow-up actions, and archive the correspondence, all without requiring manual intervention.

MAPI's notification system is another powerful feature that enhances Outlook's functionality. Applications can subscribe to specific folders, messages, or item types, receiving real-time updates when changes occur. This event-driven architecture allows organizations to build responsive systems that automatically take action when business-critical emails arrive or when appointments are rescheduled. For example, a sales team could implement a MAPI-based solution that immediately alerts the team lead when an email marked as high priority is received from a key client. These real-time notifications allow businesses to act swiftly and maintain strong relationships with customers and partners.

Security and compliance controls are also improved with MAPI's capabilities in Outlook. By automating the application of encryption policies, digital signatures, or message classifications, MAPI helps ensure that sensitive data is consistently protected according to corporate guidelines. MAPI-based workflows can automatically enforce encryption on messages containing sensitive information or apply retention tags to emails and calendar events to comply with industry regulations such as GDPR or HIPAA.

Finally, MAPI's role in Outlook extends to integration with other Microsoft services, such as SharePoint and Microsoft Teams. Custom workflows can be designed using MAPI to automatically upload Outlook attachments to SharePoint libraries, notify teams via Microsoft Teams when key messages are received, or schedule collaborative meetings directly from shared calendars. This seamless integration strengthens Outlook's position as a central hub for enterprise collaboration, enabling users to move effortlessly between email, document management, and team-based communication platforms.

By going beyond basic email and calendar functions, MAPI transforms Outlook into a powerful platform for business process automation, custom application development, and enterprise integration. Its robust API set provides organizations with the tools needed to optimize workflows, improve user productivity, and deliver tailored solutions that address industry-specific requirements. MAPI with Outlook unlocks capabilities that make messaging and collaboration not just efficient but deeply aligned with the organization's strategic and operational goals.

Integrating MAPI with Modern Collaboration Tools

The evolving landscape of business communication has seen a significant shift from isolated messaging systems to integrated collaboration platforms that combine email, chat, video conferencing, file sharing, and project management. MAPI, or Messaging Application Programming Interface, has traditionally served as the backbone for email and calendar integration with Microsoft Exchange and Outlook. However, as organizations increasingly adopt modern collaboration tools such as Microsoft Teams, Slack, SharePoint, and other cloud-based solutions, the integration of MAPI into these platforms has become a critical enabler of unified communication workflows. MAPI's flexibility allows businesses to bridge the gap between legacy email-based processes and modern collaboration ecosystems, creating seamless and efficient workflows across diverse teams and technologies.

One of the most common integrations between MAPI and modern collaboration tools is the combination of Outlook and Microsoft Teams. Many organizations rely on Outlook for email and calendar management, while Teams serves as the central hub for chat, file sharing, and virtual meetings. MAPI plays a crucial role in linking these two platforms by providing the underlying API functionality needed to automate scheduling, message routing, and meeting management. For example, when a user creates a Teams meeting directly from Outlook using the Teams add-in, MAPI facilitates the creation of the calendar event in Exchange, attaches the meeting link, and distributes the invitation to all participants. This integration ensures that employees do not need to switch between multiple applications to schedule virtual meetings or track participant responses, streamlining the collaboration process.

MAPI also supports the integration of Outlook email workflows with persistent chat platforms like Microsoft Teams or Slack. In many enterprises, important project updates or client communications still originate via email, but actionable insights and discussions happen in chat channels. MAPI enables developers to build connectors that monitor specific Outlook folders or mailboxes and automatically post email contents or summaries into designated Teams or Slack channels. For example, a customer support team may use a MAPI-integrated bot to forward urgent client emails from a shared mailbox directly into a Teams channel, where the team can quickly collaborate on a response. This cross-platform integration improves response times, promotes transparency, and ensures that critical information does not remain siloed within individual inboxes.

Another key area where MAPI enhances collaboration tools is through its integration with document management systems like SharePoint or OneDrive. Email remains a primary medium for document exchange, but storing and managing these files in Outlook alone can lead to inefficiencies. By integrating MAPI with SharePoint, organizations can automate the process of extracting email attachments and uploading them to centralized document libraries. For instance, a sales operations team could implement a workflow where contracts received via email are automatically saved to a secure SharePoint folder, tagged with metadata such as client name and deal stage. This not only reduces manual file handling but also ensures that documents are properly categorized, version-controlled, and accessible to all relevant stakeholders through SharePoint's collaboration features.

MAPI further enables collaboration by supporting task automation between Outlook and project management platforms such as Microsoft Planner, Asana, or Trello. Through MAPI, businesses can automate the creation of tasks in these platforms based on triggers from email and calendar events in Outlook. For example, when a project manager receives an email confirming the completion of a project milestone, a MAPI-based integration could automatically create follow-up tasks in Planner, assign them to team members, and link the related email thread for reference. This integration minimizes manual data entry, enhances task visibility, and helps ensure that project workflows are consistently tracked and managed across tools.

Calendar synchronization is another essential use case where MAPI extends the capabilities of modern collaboration tools. Many organizations operate in environments where scheduling is distributed between Outlook calendars and project management tools that have their own event tracking systems. MAPI allows for automated synchronization between Outlook and these platforms, ensuring that calendar events created in one system are reflected in the other. This is particularly valuable for organizations coordinating meetings, deadlines, or resource bookings across multifunctional teams. For instance, a product development team might schedule project sprints and retrospectives in a project management tool, and MAPI ensures these events are mirrored in team members' Outlook calendars to avoid scheduling conflicts and keep everyone aligned.

In regulated industries, where compliance and data protection are critical, MAPI's integration with collaboration tools supports the enforcement of security and governance policies. For example, organizations can use MAPI to enforce email encryption or apply sensitivity labels before automating the sharing of information with external collaboration tools. If a confidential client email is to be shared in a Teams channel, a MAPI-enabled process can ensure that only approved users have access, and that messages containing sensitive data are flagged or restricted according to internal compliance rules. MAPI also facilitates audit logging and retention management by ensuring that messages and documents routed through collaboration tools are properly archived and meet regulatory standards.

MAPI plays a significant role in enhancing mobile collaboration experiences as well. As more employees rely on mobile devices to access Outlook and modern collaboration platforms, MAPI over HTTP ensures that the integration between messaging systems and collaboration tools functions securely and efficiently from any location. For example, an executive working remotely can receive an important client email on their Outlook mobile app and, thanks to MAPI-based automation, see the same information posted to the relevant Teams channel or project board on their mobile device in near real-time. This enables faster decision-making and facilitates immediate collaboration, regardless of where employees are located.

MAPI's extensibility also supports the development of custom integrations between Outlook and industry-specific collaboration tools. Organizations in sectors such as healthcare, finance, or legal services often require specialized platforms to manage client records, case files, or regulatory documents. MAPI enables these organizations to integrate Outlook-based communication workflows with proprietary collaboration systems. For example, a legal firm could use MAPI to automate the transfer of client correspondence from Outlook to a case management platform, ensuring that every client interaction is logged and accessible to legal teams working collaboratively on the case.

The combination of MAPI and modern collaboration tools empowers businesses to break down silos between email-centric workflows and broader team collaboration activities. By integrating messaging, calendaring, document management, and task coordination into a unified ecosystem, MAPI ensures that employees can move seamlessly between communication channels and productivity tools. This leads to improved workflow efficiency, faster response times, and a more cohesive collaboration experience across the organization.

As modern workplaces continue to evolve, MAPI will remain a critical enabler of integrated communication strategies, allowing organizations to leverage both traditional and next-generation collaboration platforms. The ability to automate, synchronize, and secure communication workflows through MAPI ensures that businesses can respond to changing work dynamics while maintaining control and consistency across their enterprise collaboration tools.

MAPI and AI-Powered Business Communications

The convergence of MAPI, or Messaging Application Programming Interface, with artificial intelligence (AI) is transforming business communications into a more dynamic, intelligent, and automated experience. While MAPI has long been the standard for enabling Outlook and other client applications to interact with Microsoft

Exchange servers for email, calendaring, and task management, the integration of AI-powered technologies is now elevating MAPI-based workflows far beyond traditional messaging systems. AI brings new dimensions to how businesses leverage MAPI by enhancing automation, decision-making, data extraction, and personalized communication at scale.

At the core of this transformation is the ability of AI to analyze vast amounts of data passing through MAPI-enabled messaging systems and extract actionable insights in real time. AI models can be embedded into MAPI-based workflows to automatically process emails, identify patterns, and categorize content with a level of speed and accuracy that manual methods cannot match. For instance, when MAPI-enabled applications monitor an inbox, AI algorithms can analyze incoming emails to classify them based on urgency, sentiment, or topic, and automatically route them to the correct department or escalate high-priority messages to leadership teams. This intelligent triage capability reduces response times and ensures that critical information reaches the right stakeholders without delay.

AI integration with MAPI also empowers businesses to automate more sophisticated customer interaction workflows. By combining MAPI with natural language processing (NLP) models, organizations can build systems that understand and respond to customer inquiries directly through email. For example, when a customer sends a request for product information or technical support, an AI-powered MAPI application can automatically generate a contextual and personalized response based on the content of the inquiry, past customer interactions, and available knowledge base articles. This reduces the workload on support teams and provides customers with faster, more relevant answers.

In sales and marketing environments, the fusion of MAPI and AI is enhancing outreach and engagement strategies. AI-driven analytics tools can process email communication history stored within Exchange mailboxes accessed via MAPI, allowing sales teams to identify engagement patterns, prospect behaviors, and optimal follow-up times. MAPI-enabled applications can then automate the scheduling of follow-up emails or meeting requests based on AI recommendations. For instance, if AI detects that a prospect is more responsive to emails sent early in the week, the system can automatically schedule future communications accordingly through MAPI-integrated Outlook calendars. This data-driven approach improves engagement rates and helps sales teams focus on leads that demonstrate the highest likelihood of conversion.

MAPI and AI also intersect in the area of intelligent meeting scheduling and calendar management. AI algorithms integrated into MAPI-based workflows can analyze employees' calendars to recommend optimal meeting times, taking into consideration factors such as meeting frequency, individual workload, and historical preferences. For distributed teams operating across multiple time zones, AI can identify and suggest time slots that minimize disruptions to participants' schedules. MAPI enables these AI recommendations to be directly implemented by programmatically creating Outlook calendar events, sending meeting invites, and managing rescheduling as new priorities emerge.

AI-powered sentiment analysis is another area where MAPI plays a critical role. Organizations handling high volumes of customer or internal communication can use AI models to detect sentiment within email bodies and attachments accessed via MAPI. By flagging messages with negative sentiment, AI-enhanced MAPI workflows enable customer service or HR teams to proactively address potential conflicts, complaints, or dissatisfaction before they escalate. This capability helps organizations maintain strong customer relationships and a healthy internal work environment by identifying potential issues early through communication monitoring.

Beyond analyzing content, AI models can work with MAPI-based systems to extract structured data from unstructured email content. This is particularly valuable in industries such as finance, logistics, or legal services, where important transactional or operational data often arrives in the form of free-text emails or document attachments. AI-powered data extraction models can parse invoices, contracts, delivery notes, or compliance documents received via email, and automatically transfer the extracted information into ERP, CRM, or document management systems. MAPI enables these processes by programmatically accessing relevant messages and attachments, triggering AI-based processing workflows, and updating enterprise systems accordingly.

AI integration with MAPI is also enhancing security and compliance in business communications. AI models can be trained to detect anomalous communication patterns or potential phishing attempts within emails. When suspicious activity is identified, MAPI workflows can be designed to automatically quarantine the email, notify the security operations center, and remove similar messages from users' mailboxes. This proactive approach to cybersecurity, supported by MAPI's deep access to messaging systems, helps protect organizations against sophisticated threats and reduces reliance on reactive, manual incident response.

Additionally, AI is streamlining administrative and operational workflows within MAPI-integrated environments. Virtual assistants and AI-powered bots can interact directly with employees through Outlook, performing tasks such as automatically generating status reports, scheduling meetings, setting reminders, or retrieving key data from connected business applications. These bots leverage MAPI to access and manipulate calendar events, task lists, and emails on behalf of users, providing a more interactive and efficient user experience. For example, an AI-powered assistant could use MAPI to scan a user's inbox for project-related emails and automatically compile a summary report of project updates, deadlines, and outstanding tasks.

In customer service, AI and MAPI work together to facilitate omnichannel support experiences. While MAPI ensures that email remains an integral channel within support workflows, AI systems unify communication streams by analyzing data from email, chat, voice, and other channels. AI models can correlate data from MAPI-accessed mailboxes with ticketing systems, CRM platforms, and live chat transcripts to provide agents with a 360-degree view of customer interactions. This comprehensive insight allows support teams to deliver personalized and consistent service across all communication touchpoints.

AI-powered translation and transcription services integrated with MAPI workflows are enhancing global communication as well. When businesses operate across diverse regions and languages, MAPI-based applications can access incoming emails and automatically trigger AI services to translate the content or transcribe attached audio files. The translated messages can then be automatically distributed to relevant recipients, ensuring that language barriers do not impede productivity or collaboration.

The integration of AI with MAPI is ultimately driving the evolution of messaging systems into intelligent communication platforms. MAPI provides the essential link between AI engines and enterprise messaging data, enabling organizations to apply machine learning models directly within their communication workflows. Whether it is automating repetitive tasks, extracting actionable insights, enhancing customer engagement, or improving decision-making, the combination of AI and MAPI is redefining how businesses leverage email and calendar systems to operate more efficiently, intelligently, and competitively in a data-driven world.

Monitoring and Logging MAPI Communications

Monitoring and logging MAPI communications has become a critical practice for organizations that rely on MAPI-based applications and workflows to manage business communications. MAPI, or Messaging Application Programming Interface, serves as a vital link between client applications like Microsoft Outlook and Microsoft Exchange servers, handling sensitive business processes such as email exchanges, calendar scheduling, contact management, and task automation. Given the significance of these operations and their role in supporting collaboration and information flow within an enterprise, organizations must implement effective monitoring and logging mechanisms to ensure system integrity, troubleshoot issues, maintain compliance, and optimize performance.

At the most basic level, monitoring MAPI communications involves capturing details about client-server interactions, including session initiation, API calls, data access, and transactional activity. MAPI is deeply integrated into Microsoft Exchange, and as such, Exchange server logging provides a wealth of data related to MAPI traffic. Exchange generates protocol-level logs for MAPI over HTTP communications, which record connection attempts, authentication events, session lifecycles, and data transfer metrics. These logs are invaluable to system administrators who need to diagnose issues such as failed logins, unexpected session drops, or network bottlenecks impacting Outlook clients or custom MAPI-enabled applications.

For more detailed application-level monitoring, MAPI provides diagnostic interfaces and logging capabilities through its development libraries. Developers building custom MAPI applications can enable verbose logging to capture API calls, input parameters, and response codes. By analyzing this data, development teams can pinpoint inefficient API usage, detect failed operations, and optimize code execution. This granular view into the internal workings of MAPI applications helps reduce latency, identify programming errors, and ensure that messaging operations are executed as intended.

One of the most common challenges addressed by MAPI communication monitoring is the detection and resolution of performance issues affecting client applications. When users report slow Outlook performance, delayed message delivery, or intermittent connectivity problems, MAPI logs often provide the critical clues needed to identify root causes. Exchange administrators can analyze MAPI over HTTP logs to review connection timings, identify authentication errors, and observe how long it takes clients to retrieve mailbox data. For example, if logs show that MAPI sessions frequently encounter timeout errors or connection resets, this may point to underlying network issues, overloaded servers, or client-side misconfigurations.

In addition to troubleshooting performance, logging MAPI communications is essential for maintaining security and enforcing compliance. Many industries, such as finance, healthcare, and legal services, operate under strict regulatory frameworks that require detailed audit trails of all communication activities, including email traffic and mailbox access. By logging MAPI sessions, organizations can track who accessed which messaging objects, when, and from which device or IP address. This level of transparency allows security teams to detect unauthorized access attempts, unusual behavior patterns, and potential data breaches.

MAPI logging also plays a critical role in supporting incident response and forensic investigations. In the event of a security incident, such as a phishing attack or data exfiltration attempt, forensic teams can leverage MAPI logs to reconstruct the sequence of events, analyze how malicious actors accessed and manipulated messaging data, and determine the scope of the breach. By correlating MAPI logs with other security logs, such as firewall, endpoint detection, or Active Directory logs, organizations can gain a holistic understanding of the incident and take appropriate corrective actions.

Proactive monitoring of MAPI communications goes beyond basic logging by leveraging real-time analytics and alerting systems. Many enterprises integrate MAPI log data with security information and event management (SIEM) platforms, such as Splunk or Microsoft Sentinel, to continuously analyze patterns and generate alerts based on predefined thresholds or anomalous behavior. For instance, if an unusually high volume of MAPI session initiations occurs within a short period, or if a user account accesses an abnormally large number of mailboxes, automated alerts can notify IT security teams for immediate investigation. This real-time monitoring capability helps prevent small issues from escalating into larger security or operational problems.

Exchange administrators can also utilize tools such as the Microsoft Exchange Diagnostic Logging feature, which provides configurable logging levels for various Exchange components, including MAPI. By adjusting the logging granularity, administrators can balance the need for detailed diagnostics with system performance and storage considerations. For example, during normal operations, organizations may opt for standard logging to capture high-level metrics, but when troubleshooting specific issues, they can temporarily enable verbose logging to capture more detailed data on MAPI API calls and session activity.

Another key aspect of monitoring MAPI communications is tracking mailbox audit logs, which record actions taken by users, administrators, and delegated accounts within mailboxes. When

MAPI-enabled applications or Outlook clients perform operations such as sending emails, creating calendar appointments, or modifying mailbox permissions, these actions are recorded and stored according to the organization's retention policies. Administrators can review these logs to validate user activity, enforce compliance with internal policies, and respond to regulatory audits.

Custom MAPI-based applications benefit from implementing their own logging mechanisms to capture application-specific events and outcomes. For example, a MAPI-enabled customer support application that automatically processes incoming emails can generate logs detailing how messages are routed, categorized, and processed. These application-level logs complement server-side MAPI logs and provide end-to-end visibility into business-critical workflows. Developers can design these logs to include contextual information, such as customer IDs, case numbers, or workflow status, to facilitate root cause analysis and continuous improvement.

In hybrid environments where organizations maintain both on-premises Exchange servers and Exchange Online mailboxes, monitoring MAPI communications across both infrastructures becomes increasingly complex. To address this, businesses often implement unified monitoring solutions that consolidate log data from multiple environments into a centralized dashboard. This unified view enables IT teams to identify trends, detect inconsistencies, and ensure that hybrid MAPI communications meet the organization's performance, security, and compliance standards.

Finally, continuous monitoring and logging of MAPI communications contribute to optimizing resource allocation and capacity planning. By analyzing historical log data, administrators can identify patterns in user activity, such as peak periods of MAPI traffic, mailbox usage trends, or growing demands on public folders and shared mailboxes. This information supports data-driven decisions on server scaling, network upgrades, or infrastructure optimizations that improve the overall performance and reliability of MAPI-based services.

Monitoring and logging MAPI communications are foundational practices that ensure enterprise messaging systems remain secure, efficient, and aligned with business objectives. By capturing detailed insights into MAPI interactions, organizations gain the ability to troubleshoot issues, enforce compliance, respond to security incidents, and optimize communication workflows in complex, evolving IT environments.

MAPI Performance Tuning for Large Enterprises

As large enterprises scale their messaging environments to support thousands of users, departments, and business processes, ensuring optimal performance of MAPI-based systems becomes essential. MAPI, or Messaging Application Programming Interface, is a critical communication protocol that connects client applications like Microsoft Outlook with Microsoft Exchange servers to manage emails, calendars, tasks, contacts, and more. In large-scale environments, where messaging workloads can become highly complex, performance tuning of MAPI is vital to maintain system responsiveness, reduce latency, and ensure that employees experience seamless access to essential communication tools.

One of the foundational elements of MAPI performance tuning in large enterprises is optimizing MAPI over HTTP, which is the modern transport protocol used by MAPI clients to communicate with Exchange servers. MAPI over HTTP offers improved reliability and resiliency compared to legacy protocols like RPC over HTTP, but its performance is still highly dependent on network infrastructure, server configuration, and client behavior. To maximize throughput and minimize session-related bottlenecks, administrators must ensure that network bandwidth is sufficient to handle peak MAPI traffic volumes. This includes optimizing internal network paths between client machines and Exchange servers, reducing latency through load balancing, and ensuring that network devices such as firewalls and proxies are configured to efficiently handle HTTPS traffic generated by MAPI over HTTP sessions.

Load balancing is particularly crucial in large enterprise environments where multiple Exchange servers are deployed to distribute MAPI traffic. An effective load balancing strategy ensures that incoming client requests are evenly distributed across available servers, preventing overload on individual servers and maintaining consistent response times. Load balancers should be configured to support session persistence, also known as client affinity, to ensure that MAPI sessions are consistently routed to the same Exchange server during the session lifecycle, minimizing session re-establishment overhead and reducing the potential for session interruptions.

Another key area of focus for MAPI performance tuning is optimizing Exchange server hardware and resource allocation. In large enterprises, Exchange servers must be equipped with sufficient CPU, memory, and disk I/O capacity to handle high volumes of concurrent MAPI connections and data transactions. Performance tuning involves monitoring server resource utilization during peak usage periods and adjusting hardware configurations accordingly. This may include increasing memory allocation to support larger mailbox databases, deploying faster storage systems to reduce disk latency, and ensuring that server CPUs can efficiently process the load generated by MAPI calls, background tasks, and transaction logs.

Exchange database optimization is also a critical component of MAPI performance tuning. As MAPI interacts with mailbox databases to read and write messages, calendar items, and other data, database performance directly impacts the user experience. Administrators should implement best practices for database maintenance, including regular defragmentation, index optimization, and appropriate mailbox database sizing. Large mailbox databases should be segmented into smaller, more manageable units to reduce contention and improve overall read/write performance. Additionally, enabling features such as Data Availability Groups (DAG) ensures high availability and load distribution across Exchange servers.

Client-side performance optimization is another essential factor in tuning MAPI performance for large enterprises. Outlook clients, which are the primary consumers of MAPI services, can experience performance degradation if not properly configured. For example, clients with large offline storage files (OST) can exhibit slow folder switching, search delays, and synchronization issues. Administrators can mitigate these issues by implementing policies to limit the size of

OST files, such as enabling Cached Exchange Mode but restricting offline storage to emails from the past six or twelve months. This reduces the local data footprint and improves Outlook performance without compromising access to recent or frequently used information.

MAPI performance tuning also extends to mailbox management practices. In large enterprises, users often accumulate vast amounts of email data, leading to bloated mailboxes that impact both client and server performance. To address this, organizations should enforce mailbox quotas and encourage archiving practices that move older or less critical data to archive mailboxes or dedicated storage systems. Automated retention policies can also be implemented to systematically clean up outdated messages and free up resources within the Exchange environment.

Advanced MAPI applications and custom workflows developed by enterprises must be designed with performance in mind. Developers should adhere to MAPI development best practices, such as minimizing the use of high-cost API calls, reducing the number of round trips to the server, and implementing efficient error-handling routines to prevent failed transactions from causing system slowdowns. Applications that automate processes such as email routing, appointment scheduling, or task management should be designed to batch-process data whenever possible, rather than initiating a separate MAPI session or transaction for each individual item.

Monitoring and proactive alerting are integral to effective MAPI performance tuning in large organizations. By implementing robust monitoring tools, such as Exchange Health Manager or third-party performance management platforms, administrators can collect real-time data on key metrics such as session establishment times, server response times, resource usage, and error rates. Threshold-based alerting enables teams to detect performance anomalies, such as spikes in MAPI session failures or unusual load patterns, and take corrective actions before they escalate into service outages or widespread performance degradation.

Capacity planning is also a critical consideration for enterprises seeking to maintain optimal MAPI performance as they scale. Based on monitoring data and usage trends, IT teams must regularly review resource utilization forecasts and plan for hardware upgrades, Exchange server scaling, or adjustments to network capacity. This ensures that the MAPI infrastructure is prepared to handle seasonal increases in workload, organizational growth, or changes in business operations, such as the onboarding of large numbers of new employees or the launch of new applications that rely on MAPI services.

In hybrid environments where enterprises operate both on-premises Exchange servers and Exchange Online mailboxes within Microsoft 365, tuning MAPI performance requires additional attention to the interaction between local infrastructure and cloud services. Hybrid deployments often involve complex routing configurations, hybrid identity management, and coexistence between legacy applications and modern cloud-native tools. Ensuring that MAPI communications between on-premises and cloud-hosted mailboxes are optimized requires close coordination between Exchange administrators, network engineers, and cloud architects.

Ultimately, MAPI performance tuning in large enterprises is an ongoing process that requires continuous refinement, monitoring, and adaptation. By combining infrastructure optimization, application design best practices, proactive maintenance, and capacity planning, organizations can ensure that their MAPI-enabled environments remain responsive, scalable, and capable of supporting critical communication workflows at enterprise scale. MAPI's role as the backbone of email and collaboration infrastructure makes its performance optimization a strategic priority for businesses committed to delivering reliable and efficient messaging services to their employees.

Disaster Recovery and MAPI

Disaster recovery is a fundamental component of business continuity planning, ensuring that critical systems and services can be restored quickly following unexpected disruptions. In modern enterprises, where email and messaging are essential to daily operations, MAPI, or Messaging Application Programming Interface, plays a crucial role in maintaining resilience and operational continuity. MAPI acts as the communication layer between client applications like Microsoft Outlook and Microsoft Exchange servers, facilitating the flow of information across emails, calendars, contacts, and tasks. When a disaster strikes, organizations must have comprehensive recovery strategies that ensure MAPI-enabled communication services are restored with minimal downtime, preserving both the availability of messaging systems and the integrity of business-critical data.

The reliance on MAPI for essential business workflows means that any outage or disruption to Exchange servers or supporting infrastructure can severely impact communication and collaboration across an organization. Whether caused by hardware failure, network outages, cyberattacks, or natural disasters, such disruptions can prevent employees from accessing their mailboxes, delay critical communications, and hinder productivity. Therefore, disaster recovery strategies for MAPI environments must focus on several key areas: data protection, failover capabilities, service redundancy, and rapid recovery procedures.

A cornerstone of disaster recovery in MAPI-enabled environments is the use of Exchange Database Availability Groups (DAGs). DAGs provide high availability and site resilience for mailbox databases by replicating data across multiple Exchange servers located in separate physical sites or data centers. In the event of a server failure or site outage, the DAG automatically initiates failover processes, promoting passive database copies to active status and redirecting MAPI traffic to available servers. This ensures that Outlook clients and MAPI-enabled applications can continue to access mailboxes without interruption, even during localized infrastructure failures. DAGs are configured to synchronize database copies in near real time, preserving the integrity of messaging data and reducing the risk of data loss.

MAPI performance is directly tied to the health of Exchange infrastructure, making redundancy at every layer critical for disaster recovery. Enterprises should implement redundant load balancers, network paths, and storage systems to ensure that MAPI traffic can be rerouted in the event of a failure. Load balancers should be configured with health probes that detect the availability of Exchange Client Access Services and dynamically adjust routing based on server health. This allows MAPI sessions to automatically reconnect to healthy servers, maintaining user access and minimizing the impact of backend server outages.

Another key consideration in disaster recovery planning is the protection of the offline data used by MAPI clients, particularly Outlook OST (Offline Storage Table) files. In environments where Cached Exchange Mode is enabled, users rely on OST files to access mailbox data while offline. Organizations should ensure that endpoint backup strategies include regular backups of user profiles and OST files, so data can be recovered in scenarios where local devices are compromised or lost. This is especially important for remote or field employees who may not have consistent access to live Exchange servers during a disaster scenario.

Backup and restore capabilities for Exchange servers are central to disaster recovery for MAPI environments. Regular, automated backups of Exchange mailbox databases, public folders, and configuration settings are critical to ensure data can be restored quickly in the event of corruption, accidental deletion, or a catastrophic system failure. Backups should be stored both on-site and off-site, with consideration given to cloud-based backup solutions that provide geographically redundant storage. Enterprises should routinely test restore procedures to validate that backups can be used to quickly rebuild Exchange servers and recover mailboxes while maintaining MAPI functionality.

Hybrid environments introduce additional complexity to disaster recovery planning. Many organizations operate in hybrid models where some mailboxes are hosted on-premises while others reside in Exchange Online as part of Microsoft 365. In such scenarios, MAPI disaster recovery strategies must account for both local infrastructure resilience and cloud service continuity. Microsoft provides service-level agreements (SLAs) for Exchange Online availability, but enterprises are still responsible for ensuring hybrid configurations are resilient, including maintaining the availability of on-premises directory synchronization services, hybrid connectors, and local MAPI-enabled applications that integrate with both cloud and on-premises mailboxes.

During extended outages or disaster events that impact entire data centers or regions, organizations may activate business continuity plans that include switching operations to secondary or disaster recovery sites. MAPI disaster recovery strategies should ensure that client access can be seamlessly redirected to alternative Exchange servers located in secondary sites. This requires pre-configured network routing, updated DNS records, and global load balancing configurations that enable clients to reconnect to the failover environment without requiring manual reconfiguration of Outlook profiles or custom MAPI applications.

Another aspect of MAPI disaster recovery involves ensuring application-level resilience for custom solutions built on MAPI. Many enterprises deploy MAPI-based applications for automating email routing, monitoring shared mailboxes, or integrating messaging workflows with business systems such as CRM or ERP platforms. These applications should be designed to detect service outages and automatically retry operations, failover to alternative Exchange endpoints, or queue transactions for deferred processing once connectivity is restored. Properly architected applications can help maintain business continuity by preserving transactional integrity and preventing data loss during periods of reduced system availability.

Post-disaster recovery testing and validation are critical to ensuring that MAPI-enabled services are fully operational following the restoration of systems. Once Exchange servers, databases, and network infrastructure are brought back online, IT teams should perform comprehensive validation checks to confirm that MAPI sessions can be successfully established, mailboxes are accessible, calendar synchronization is functional, and automated workflows resume as expected. User experience testing is also essential to verify that Outlook clients and MAPI-based applications are operating normally across distributed teams.

Communication and documentation are essential components of an effective disaster recovery plan. Clear communication protocols should be established to keep stakeholders informed during outages, detailing expected recovery timelines and providing alternative contact methods when MAPI services are unavailable. IT teams should maintain detailed disaster recovery runbooks that outline each step of the recovery process, including procedures for restoring Exchange databases, re-establishing MAPI session connectivity, and validating business-critical messaging services.

Ultimately, MAPI's role in disaster recovery extends beyond technical resilience to supporting the continuity of business operations, collaboration, and customer engagement. By implementing robust disaster recovery strategies that leverage Exchange DAGs, redundant infrastructure, reliable backups, and resilient application designs, enterprises can safeguard MAPI-enabled services and reduce the operational impact of unforeseen disruptions. Ensuring that communication remains accessible and reliable under any circumstance is a strategic priority for organizations that depend on MAPI-driven messaging ecosystems to support their day-to-day operations and long-term success.

Best Practices for MAPI Deployment

Deploying MAPI, or Messaging Application Programming Interface, in an enterprise environment requires a thoughtful and methodical approach to ensure optimal performance, security, and long-term maintainability. MAPI acts as a critical interface between client applications, most notably Microsoft Outlook, and Microsoft Exchange servers, enabling essential business functions such as email communication, calendar scheduling, contact management, and task automation. While MAPI provides a powerful set of capabilities, its deployment must adhere to industry best practices to fully leverage its potential and minimize the risk of operational inefficiencies or system vulnerabilities.

The first best practice for MAPI deployment is ensuring that the environment is prepared for MAPI over HTTP, the modern transport protocol used for MAPI communications. MAPI over HTTP replaces legacy RPC over HTTP, offering better reliability, faster reconnections, and improved session stability. Before deployment, administrators must verify that all Exchange servers and client applications are configured to support MAPI over HTTP, including applying the latest cumulative updates to the Exchange environment and ensuring that Outlook clients are using supported versions. Proper configuration of virtual directories on Exchange servers is critical, including the accurate setting of internal and external URLs and ensuring SSL certificates are trusted and properly installed.

Network infrastructure plays a pivotal role in successful MAPI deployment. Enterprises must assess and optimize their network to accommodate MAPI traffic, focusing on ensuring adequate bandwidth, low latency, and minimal packet loss between client endpoints and Exchange servers. Deploying load balancers to distribute client requests across multiple Exchange Client Access Servers enhances resilience and balances workloads. Configuring session persistence, or client affinity, on load balancers helps maintain session continuity and prevents issues related to session failover or interruption during active MAPI communications.

It is a best practice to implement centralized configuration management for Outlook clients to enforce consistent MAPI-related settings across the enterprise. Using Group Policy Objects (GPOs) or Microsoft Endpoint Manager, administrators can standardize client settings such as enabling Cached Exchange Mode, configuring MAPI over HTTP, setting limits on offline storage file (OST) sizes, and defining synchronization windows for cached data. Standardization helps streamline client-side performance, reduce support incidents, and ensure that all users benefit from optimized MAPI configurations.

Mailbox management is another critical area of focus when deploying MAPI in large organizations. To prevent performance degradation, administrators should enforce mailbox quotas and encourage users to archive older messages or leverage online archive mailboxes. Oversized mailboxes lead to slower synchronization times, increased load on MAPI sessions, and poor Outlook performance, particularly when operating in Cached Exchange Mode. Automated retention policies can assist in managing mailbox sizes and ensuring that data is stored according to compliance requirements.

Security best practices must be integrated into every aspect of MAPI deployment. All MAPI communications should be encrypted using SSL/TLS to protect data in transit between clients and Exchange servers. Organizations should enforce multi-factor authentication (MFA) for all user accounts to reduce the risk of unauthorized access through MAPI-enabled clients. Additionally, MAPI service accounts used by custom applications or background services should follow the principle of least privilege, limiting permissions to only what is required for operational functionality. Regular security audits should be conducted to verify that MAPI permissions and configurations adhere to internal security policies and regulatory requirements.

Monitoring and logging are essential components of a well-managed MAPI deployment. Administrators should implement tools that provide visibility into MAPI session activity, connection trends, error rates, and performance metrics. By leveraging Exchange protocol logs, monitoring platforms such as Microsoft System Center Operations Manager (SCOM), or third-party performance management tools, organizations can proactively detect and resolve issues before they impact end users. Alerting systems should be configured to notify administrators of anomalies such as excessive failed logins, session timeouts, or unexpected spikes in MAPI traffic, all of which could indicate security incidents or system misconfigurations.

For organizations with custom MAPI-based applications, developers should follow MAPI development best practices to ensure that applications operate efficiently and do not introduce unnecessary load on the Exchange infrastructure. Applications should be designed to minimize server round trips, batch-process messages when feasible, and handle error conditions gracefully. Developers should avoid long-running MAPI sessions that consume resources unnecessarily and should implement retry logic with exponential backoff to handle transient failures in a controlled manner.

When deploying MAPI in hybrid environments that include both on-premises Exchange servers and Exchange Online in Microsoft 365, administrators must ensure that hybrid configurations are properly established and tested. This includes setting up hybrid connectors, directory synchronization, and hybrid authentication mechanisms such as Azure AD Connect with Seamless Single Sign-On (SSO).

Careful attention should be paid to routing configurations to ensure that MAPI clients can seamlessly access mailboxes hosted both locally and in the cloud without user intervention or performance degradation.

It is also a best practice to plan for scalability from the outset of any MAPI deployment project. As user counts grow or as additional MAPI-based applications are introduced, Exchange servers must have sufficient capacity to handle increased concurrent connections and data throughput. Capacity planning should include assessments of CPU utilization, memory usage, disk I/O, and network bandwidth, with regular reviews to anticipate future demand. Deploying additional Client Access Servers and expanding DAG configurations may be necessary as the organization scales.

Disaster recovery planning must be incorporated into MAPI deployment strategies. Organizations should implement redundant systems, including multiple Exchange servers in geographically separate locations, to ensure messaging continuity in the event of a localized outage. Database Availability Groups (DAGs) and secondary datacenter infrastructure should be configured to provide automated failover capabilities, with regular testing to validate that failover and failback procedures work seamlessly for MAPI sessions and client connections.

Lastly, user education and support readiness are critical components of a successful MAPI deployment. End users should be provided with training materials or quick-reference guides that explain how MAPI impacts Outlook functionality, particularly when transitioning from legacy protocols to MAPI over HTTP. IT support teams should be equipped with diagnostic tools and troubleshooting playbooks tailored to resolving common MAPI-related issues such as profile corruption, synchronization delays, or connection failures.

By following these best practices, organizations can deploy MAPI effectively while ensuring a secure, scalable, and high-performing messaging environment. A properly executed MAPI deployment supports seamless communication, enhances collaboration, and enables organizations to meet the evolving demands of modern enterprise operations. From network design and server configuration to client optimization and security enforcement, every element of the MAPI deployment process contributes to building a resilient and efficient infrastructure capable of supporting business-critical communication workflows.

MAPI and Compliance with Global Regulations

As organizations increasingly rely on digital communications to conduct business, ensuring compliance with global regulations has become a top priority for enterprises operating across international borders. MAPI, or Messaging Application Programming Interface, is a key component of corporate messaging infrastructures, enabling applications like Microsoft Outlook and various business systems to interact with Exchange servers for email, calendar, contact, and task management. Because MAPI plays a direct role in handling sensitive business communications, it must be integrated into broader compliance frameworks designed to meet regulatory obligations such as the General Data Protection Regulation (GDPR), the Health Insurance Portability and Accountability Act (HIPAA), the Sarbanes-Oxley Act (SOX), and other regional data protection laws.

Compliance with global regulations begins with understanding how MAPI-based applications access, transmit, and store data. MAPI facilitates the transfer of emails, attachments, meeting invites, and related metadata between client applications and Exchange servers. This data often includes personal information, financial records, contractual documents, and proprietary business information. To ensure compliance, organizations must implement security controls that protect this data throughout its lifecycle. Encryption is a critical requirement, and MAPI communications must be secured using SSL/TLS protocols to ensure that data in transit between clients and servers cannot be intercepted or tampered with by unauthorized parties. This is particularly important for organizations subject to GDPR, which mandates that personal data be protected through appropriate technical and organizational measures.

MAPI also supports integration with Secure/Multipurpose Internet Mail Extensions (S/MIME), allowing organizations to enforce end-to-end encryption and digital signatures at the message level. For industries such as healthcare and finance, where regulations like HIPAA and SOX require strict protection of sensitive information, using MAPI in conjunction with S/MIME enables businesses to ensure that confidential data remains secure even when transmitted outside the organization's network boundaries. S/MIME further provides non-repudiation by ensuring the authenticity of message senders and the integrity of message content.

Another key compliance consideration when using MAPI is data retention and archiving. Many regulations require organizations to retain communication records for specified periods to support legal discovery, financial auditing, or regulatory investigations. For example, financial institutions subject to the Dodd-Frank Act or MiFID II regulations must retain client communications for several years. MAPI enables automated archiving workflows by allowing administrators to configure Exchange to move emails from user mailboxes to archive mailboxes or external storage systems based on retention policies. MAPI-based applications can also programmatically tag emails with retention classifications, automate the transfer of records to compliance archives, and ensure that messaging data is readily accessible for audits.

Audit logging is another crucial component of regulatory compliance in MAPI-enabled environments. MAPI interacts with Exchange mailbox audit logs and message tracking logs to capture detailed records of user activity, including who accessed or modified messaging data, when it occurred, and from where. These logs are indispensable for demonstrating compliance with regulations that require accountability and traceability of user actions. For example, under GDPR, organizations must be able to show that appropriate safeguards are in place to protect personal data, including monitoring and reporting on access to that data. MAPI enables the generation of audit logs that document interactions with sensitive communications, such as access to emails containing personal information or financial reports.

Compliance with global regulations also requires organizations to implement robust data classification and labeling processes. MAPI supports the integration of data protection technologies such as Microsoft Information Protection (MIP), which allows administrators to apply sensitivity labels to emails and documents based on content. MAPI-based workflows can automate the assignment of labels that enforce encryption, apply rights management protections, and restrict forwarding or printing. For example, emails classified as "Confidential" can be automatically encrypted and restricted from being shared with unauthorized recipients. These controls help organizations comply with regulatory mandates related to data privacy and confidentiality.

Data subject rights under GDPR, such as the right to access, rectify, or erase personal data, also have implications for MAPI-based systems. When a data subject requests access to their personal information, organizations must be able to retrieve relevant communication records quickly and accurately. MAPI enables administrators to search mailboxes, public folders, and archives for messages containing personal data, export the data as needed, and ensure it is delivered securely to the data subject. Similarly, if a right to erasure request is received, MAPI can facilitate the deletion of relevant messages across mailboxes and storage systems, while maintaining records of compliance with the request in audit logs.

Global regulations often require organizations to secure data across multiple jurisdictions, creating additional challenges for MAPI-based deployments. For example, GDPR restricts the transfer of personal data outside the European Economic Area (EEA) unless appropriate safeguards are in place. MAPI-enabled environments must be designed to respect data sovereignty requirements, ensuring that data accessed or processed through MAPI workflows remains within approved geographic boundaries. Organizations operating in hybrid or multi-cloud environments must carefully configure their Exchange and MAPI infrastructures to comply with data localization laws, using region-specific data centers and ensuring that cross-border data transfers are compliant with binding corporate rules (BCRs) or standard contractual clauses (SCCs).

Security incident detection and response is another regulatory requirement where MAPI plays a supporting role. MAPI-based systems can integrate with security information and event management (SIEM) platforms to provide real-time monitoring of messaging activities. Alerts can be generated based on predefined compliance criteria, such as unauthorized access to sensitive mailboxes, mass mailbox exports, or repeated failed login attempts. By correlating MAPI logs with security events, organizations can detect potential data breaches early and respond in accordance with regulatory timelines, such as GDPR's 72-hour breach notification requirement.

Employee awareness and training are also essential to ensuring that MAPI-enabled systems are used in compliance with global regulations. Organizations must educate employees on best practices for handling sensitive information within MAPI-integrated tools like Outlook. This includes guidance on recognizing phishing emails, applying sensitivity labels, and securely managing calendar invitations that may contain confidential information. MAPI's integration with Outlook's user interface can support these efforts by surfacing security tips, warnings, and prompts that reinforce data protection practices.

Ultimately, MAPI serves as a foundational technology in enterprise messaging infrastructures, and its role in regulatory compliance is multifaceted. It supports data encryption, retention, auditing, classification, and secure data transfer across both on-premises and cloud-hosted environments. Organizations that leverage MAPI must ensure that its implementation aligns with evolving global regulatory frameworks to avoid legal liabilities, financial penalties, and reputational damage. By embedding compliance considerations into every aspect of MAPI deployment and management, enterprises can build a secure and resilient communication system that meets regulatory expectations and fosters trust among customers, partners, and regulators alike.

Case Study: MAPI in a Multinational Corporation

When GlobalTech Solutions, a multinational corporation with over 50,000 employees operating across North America, Europe, and Asia-

Pacific, decided to overhaul its messaging and collaboration infrastructure, MAPI played a central role in the transformation. The organization faced significant challenges in unifying its fragmented communication systems, which included a mix of on-premises Exchange servers, legacy messaging platforms, and siloed collaboration tools spread across regional offices. With a growing need for global collaboration, secure communication, and business process automation, GlobalTech turned to MAPI as a foundational technology to integrate its diverse environments and ensure seamless messaging operations across borders.

At the onset of the project, GlobalTech's IT leadership identified several pain points. Different regions were using disparate versions of Exchange, and some subsidiaries were still operating legacy platforms that did not natively support modern collaboration workflows. The lack of centralized management led to inconsistent security policies, unreliable cross-office communications, and difficulty in scaling business applications that relied on messaging services. MAPI was selected as the integration layer due to its deep compatibility with Microsoft Exchange and Outlook, its support for hybrid cloud deployments, and its ability to automate key processes that would reduce manual effort across teams.

The initial phase of the deployment involved standardizing the company's messaging environment by migrating all regional offices to a hybrid Exchange model that combined on-premises Exchange servers with Microsoft 365's Exchange Online. MAPI over HTTP was configured across all regions to modernize client-server communication and improve session reliability, replacing outdated RPC over HTTP configurations that were still present in legacy environments. Load balancers were introduced at each major hub to ensure even distribution of MAPI client connections, providing redundancy and supporting GlobalTech's goal of achieving high availability for all users.

One of the critical success factors in this project was the seamless integration of Outlook with the new messaging environment through MAPI. With teams operating across time zones, the ability to maintain synchronized calendars, automate meeting scheduling, and ensure reliable email delivery was essential to day-to-day operations. MAPI enabled Outlook clients to connect effortlessly to either on-premises mailboxes or Exchange Online mailboxes, depending on the user's location and organizational role. This hybrid model ensured that executive and compliance-sensitive teams could retain control over local servers while global teams could take advantage of the flexibility and scalability offered by Exchange Online.

Beyond standard messaging functions, MAPI was used to integrate several business-critical applications with the Exchange environment. For instance, the company's global procurement system was enhanced to use MAPI for automating the approval workflow of purchase orders. When a requisition was submitted in the system, a MAPI-based process automatically generated and sent approval request emails to regional managers, attached relevant documentation, and scheduled follow-up reminders in their Outlook calendars. Once approved, the same workflow would trigger further notifications to finance teams and update shared task lists, significantly reducing processing times and improving cross-departmental transparency.

Another area where MAPI was pivotal was in streamlining customer support operations across GlobalTech's international service centers. A custom MAPI-based application was developed to monitor shared support mailboxes in different regions, automatically parsing incoming emails and generating tickets in the company's centralized helpdesk system. MAPI's ability to access message properties and attachments allowed the application to extract relevant information, classify tickets by priority or service category, and forward escalations to specialized support teams globally. This automation not only reduced manual workload for customer service representatives but also improved response times and service-level agreement adherence across multiple time zones.

GlobalTech also leveraged MAPI to improve its compliance posture in response to increasingly stringent data protection regulations. Using MAPI's integration with S/MIME and Microsoft Information Protection, sensitive emails and attachments were automatically encrypted and tagged with sensitivity labels based on predefined content policies. Additionally, MAPI workflows enabled automated archiving of email records related to financial transactions, client agreements, and regulatory communications into secure compliance storage, aligning the company's practices with global regulatory frameworks such as GDPR, SOX, and local data residency laws.

The IT team at GlobalTech placed a strong emphasis on performance tuning as part of the MAPI deployment strategy. They conducted extensive testing to optimize session management, reduce connection latency, and balance server loads across continents. MAPI logs were integrated with the company's SIEM platform to provide real-time visibility into session activity, track potential anomalies, and monitor the health of MAPI communications across hybrid environments. This proactive monitoring allowed administrators to detect and resolve issues such as session timeouts, server resource contention, and authentication delays before they could impact end-user productivity.

As a global organization, GlobalTech had to navigate the complexity of managing localized business processes while ensuring global standardization of communication protocols. MAPI's flexibility allowed the IT department to build region-specific customizations while adhering to centralized governance models. For instance, MAPI-enabled applications in Asia-Pacific were configured to integrate with local ERP systems and document management tools, while teams in Europe used MAPI workflows to enhance legal correspondence and regulatory reporting systems. Despite these localized adaptations, the core messaging infrastructure remained unified under the standardized MAPI-based Exchange environment.

Over time, GlobalTech observed significant improvements in both operational efficiency and collaboration. Teams that previously struggled with inconsistent calendar synchronization or disjointed communication channels now had a unified messaging experience, powered by MAPI's seamless integration with Exchange and Outlook. Automated workflows reduced manual tasks, freed up IT resources, and empowered departments to focus on strategic initiatives rather than troubleshooting routine communication issues.

The successful deployment of MAPI within GlobalTech's multinational environment demonstrated the value of a unified, adaptable, and scalable messaging infrastructure. By leveraging MAPI's capabilities, the company was able to modernize its email and collaboration systems, automate cross-functional workflows, and maintain compliance with global regulations. The case of GlobalTech Solutions highlights how MAPI can serve as a critical enabler for multinational corporations aiming to drive digital transformation and optimize communication across distributed teams.

Case Study: MAPI in a Small to Medium Business

When BrightWave Consulting, a growing small to medium-sized business (SMB) specializing in marketing and brand strategy, decided to expand its operations beyond its local market, it became clear that its existing communication tools were no longer sufficient. With approximately 150 employees spread across three regional offices and a growing number of remote workers, the company faced mounting challenges in maintaining seamless communication and collaboration across teams. Email exchanges were inconsistent, project deadlines were often missed due to poor scheduling visibility, and client communications were being handled through fragmented tools that lacked integration with the company's internal workflows. BrightWave's leadership recognized the need to deploy a more reliable and automated communication system to support its expansion plans. After evaluating several options, the company chose to integrate Microsoft Exchange with Outlook, leveraging MAPI, or Messaging Application Programming Interface, to provide a unified, automated, and secure messaging platform.

Prior to implementing MAPI, BrightWave relied on a mix of free email services and on-premises file sharing for day-to-day operations. While this approach sufficed in the company's early days, it quickly became a bottleneck as the team expanded. Employees regularly struggled with scheduling conflicts, as different teams used separate calendar tools with no centralized view of team availability. Important client communications were sometimes lost in personal inboxes, leading to delays and occasional project setbacks. The company's leadership decided to migrate to Microsoft Exchange Online as part of its Microsoft 365 adoption while leveraging MAPI to enable advanced integration between Outlook clients and the Exchange environment.

The initial deployment phase focused on configuring MAPI over HTTP to provide secure and reliable access to Exchange mailboxes for all employees, whether they worked in-office or remotely. By configuring Outlook clients to connect through MAPI, the company ensured consistent synchronization of emails, calendars, contacts, and tasks across the organization. Employees immediately benefited from features such as shared calendars and global address lists, which enabled them to coordinate meetings more effectively and reduce the back-and-forth typically associated with scheduling across time zones.

Beyond improving day-to-day messaging, MAPI played a pivotal role in automating key business processes. BrightWave implemented a custom MAPI-based solution to automate its client onboarding workflow. When a new project was initiated, the system automatically generated a series of Outlook tasks assigned to relevant departments, such as creative, analytics, and account management. The tasks were tied to specific milestones in the client engagement lifecycle, with deadlines and dependencies clearly outlined in Outlook task lists. Additionally, MAPI allowed the system to automatically schedule client kickoff meetings by integrating with shared calendars, ensuring that both internal teams and clients were aligned from the outset. This automation drastically reduced onboarding times and ensured that all stakeholders were aware of their responsibilities without requiring manual follow-ups from project managers.

Another area where MAPI delivered significant value was in BrightWave's client communication and reporting workflows. The company's marketing specialists frequently send campaign reports, creative proposals, and performance summaries to clients via email. To improve consistency and efficiency, BrightWave developed a MAPI-enabled application that automates the generation and distribution of client-facing reports. The application pulls data from BrightWave's analytics platforms and CRM system, formats it according to client-specific templates, and generates personalized email drafts in Outlook. Account managers review and approve these drafts before they are automatically sent to clients with the appropriate attachments and branding. This automation not only saved considerable time for account managers but also improved the professional appearance and timeliness of client communications.

Security and compliance were also key drivers behind BrightWave's decision to leverage MAPI. As the company began working with larger clients, including those in the financial and healthcare sectors, it needed to demonstrate that it could meet industry-standard security practices. MAPI's integration with Microsoft Exchange Online's built-in security features allowed BrightWave to enforce encrypted communication protocols, apply retention policies to client correspondence, and monitor mailbox access logs to ensure that sensitive data was handled responsibly. Additionally, MAPI workflows were configured to automatically flag outgoing emails containing specific keywords or attachments for additional review by the compliance team before release.

One of the unexpected benefits of MAPI deployment was the improvement in internal collaboration across departments. Previously, BrightWave's creative and analytics teams operated in silos, often duplicating efforts or missing opportunities to share valuable insights on client projects. By centralizing communication through Outlook and leveraging MAPI to integrate shared mailboxes and public folders, teams gained better visibility into project discussions, deliverables, and client feedback. Public folders became repositories for project documentation, feedback loops were automated through MAPI-enabled workflows, and teams could easily access conversation histories and shared files without having to rely on informal channels such as chat apps or personal email threads.

BrightWave also prioritized monitoring and performance optimization during the MAPI deployment. By leveraging Exchange Online's reporting tools and MAPI's diagnostic logging, the IT team gained visibility into usage trends, connection health, and potential areas of improvement. For example, the team noticed that remote workers in regions with slower internet connections experienced occasional latency issues during peak hours. By fine-tuning Outlook caching settings, reducing unnecessary add-ins, and optimizing MAPI configurations for remote users, the IT department improved the user experience and minimized downtime for employees working outside corporate offices.

As BrightWave continued to expand its client base and open new regional offices, the scalability of its MAPI-enabled environment proved critical. The flexibility of MAPI allowed the company to integrate additional business applications with its Exchange environment, including time-tracking systems, HR onboarding platforms, and resource scheduling tools. These integrations streamlined administrative processes and helped BrightWave maintain operational agility as its workforce grew.

For BrightWave Consulting, the deployment of MAPI served as more than just a technical upgrade; it became a catalyst for operational excellence. By consolidating communication channels, automating key workflows, and ensuring secure messaging practices, the company was able to improve collaboration, enhance client satisfaction, and support its continued growth into new markets. The success of MAPI within BrightWave's SMB environment underscores how even smaller organizations can leverage enterprise-grade communication technologies to unlock efficiency and achieve competitive advantage without incurring the complexities typically associated with larger corporate environments.

Future Trends in Business Communication Integration

As technology continues to evolve at a rapid pace, the landscape of business communication is undergoing a profound transformation. Organizations are increasingly moving beyond traditional siloed communication systems and embracing integrated solutions that unify messaging, collaboration, automation, and data analytics. The future of business communication integration is shaped by several converging trends that are set to redefine how businesses connect, collaborate, and deliver value in an increasingly digital and globalized world. From artificial intelligence to cloud-native architectures, and from hybrid work models to real-time communication platforms, these trends are fundamentally changing how businesses design their communication strategies.

One of the most significant trends driving business communication integration is the rise of artificial intelligence and machine learning.

AI-powered communication platforms are increasingly capable of automating routine tasks, providing intelligent recommendations, and analyzing communication patterns to drive actionable insights. In the near future, AI will be deeply embedded within enterprise messaging systems, enabling features such as predictive email drafting, automated customer service responses, and real-time sentiment analysis of communication streams. AI will also enhance collaboration tools by suggesting optimal meeting times based on participants' past behavior, automatically summarizing meeting notes, and even detecting communication gaps within project teams to improve productivity.

The move toward unified communication and collaboration platforms is another defining trend. Enterprises are consolidating disparate communication tools into centralized hubs that integrate email, voice, video conferencing, chat, and document management. Platforms like Microsoft Teams, Slack, and Google Workspace exemplify this shift, providing seamless workflows that combine synchronous and asynchronous communication in a single interface. As APIs and integration frameworks become more robust, businesses will increasingly link these platforms with critical systems such as ERP, CRM, and workflow automation engines, creating end-to-end solutions where messages, tasks, and business data flow freely and contextually across applications.

Cloud-native architectures are further accelerating the shift towards integrated business communications. The growing adoption of Software-as-a-Service (SaaS) models enables organizations to deploy scalable, flexible communication systems without the constraints of on-premises hardware. Cloud-based platforms not only provide global accessibility but also facilitate automatic updates, improved security, and simplified integration with third-party applications. As enterprises transition toward multi-cloud and hybrid cloud strategies, business communication tools will need to operate seamlessly across cloud providers and environments. This will encourage the development of cloud-agnostic APIs and integration layers that support interoperability while maintaining consistent user experiences across different infrastructures.

The evolution of communication protocols and standards is playing a vital role in shaping the future of business communication integration. Technologies such as WebRTC are enabling real-time voice and video communication directly within web browsers and applications, eliminating the need for standalone conferencing tools. Similarly, protocols like MAPI continue to evolve in cloud-first environments, enabling secure and efficient integration between email clients and messaging servers. These developments support the broader trend of embedding communication functions directly into business applications, creating more efficient workflows where users can initiate calls, send messages, or schedule meetings from within the applications they use every day.

Hybrid and remote work models are further influencing the integration of business communication systems. With distributed teams becoming the norm, organizations are prioritizing tools that foster real-time collaboration, maintain engagement, and bridge geographic divides. Virtual collaboration platforms are being enhanced with features such as persistent chat channels, integrated file-sharing capabilities, virtual whiteboarding, and project management tools. Furthermore, communication tools are being designed to support asynchronous work, enabling employees to collaborate effectively across time zones through recorded video messages, shared task boards, and automatically generated meeting transcripts.

Another emerging trend is the emphasis on data privacy and regulatory compliance within integrated communication ecosystems. As businesses operate across regions with varying data protection laws such as GDPR, CCPA, and emerging AI regulations, communication platforms must embed compliance capabilities directly into their workflows. Future business communication tools will feature built-in data classification, automated encryption, data residency controls, and advanced auditing functions to ensure that communication streams remain secure and compliant. Additionally, AI-driven compliance tools will be able to monitor and flag communication patterns or content that violate internal policies or regulatory standards.

The integration of communication systems with business analytics and intelligence platforms is also gaining momentum. As organizations seek to make data-driven decisions, communication metadata is becoming a valuable resource. By integrating communication platforms with business intelligence tools, companies can derive insights into collaboration patterns, team productivity, customer sentiment, and engagement levels. Predictive analytics will allow organizations to identify trends and proactively address communication bottlenecks, resource allocation inefficiencies, or customer service gaps. For instance, sales teams will benefit from AI models that analyze email and meeting activity to predict deal closure likelihoods and recommend the next best actions.

Hyper-personalization is another key trend shaping the future of business communications. Leveraging AI and customer data platforms, communication tools will enable businesses to deliver highly tailored content, messages, and engagement strategies across channels. Whether through personalized marketing emails, custom onboarding sequences for new clients, or AI-driven content recommendations in customer portals, businesses will be able to strengthen relationships and increase customer satisfaction through relevant and timely communications.

Integration of communication platforms with Internet of Things (IoT) devices is another developing trend. In industries such as manufacturing, healthcare, and logistics, IoT-enabled communication will allow devices to automatically send alerts, maintenance updates, or operational data to relevant stakeholders. For example, an IoT-enabled machine on a factory floor could trigger a real-time notification via a unified communication platform when a fault is detected, instantly alerting maintenance teams and enabling quicker resolution. As IoT adoption grows, businesses will increasingly rely on integrated communication platforms to facilitate machine-to-human interactions in real time.

Finally, the future of business communication integration will also be shaped by the growing importance of immersive technologies such as augmented reality (AR) and virtual reality (VR). These technologies will expand how teams collaborate, conduct remote training, or engage with customers. Integrated AR and VR communication platforms will allow employees to collaborate in virtual environments, simulate complex tasks, or deliver remote assistance with real-time visual guidance. These innovations will redefine how teams interact, particularly in fields such as engineering, medical services, and product design, where spatial collaboration is critical.

In the coming years, the intersection of AI, cloud computing, unified communication, and advanced integration frameworks will continue to drive innovation in how businesses communicate and collaborate. Enterprises will increasingly adopt holistic, intelligent, and secure communication ecosystems designed to improve operational efficiency, enhance customer experiences, and support agile decision-making across all levels of the organization. As these trends converge, the role of communication tools will shift from being simply enablers of conversation to becoming strategic platforms that actively shape business outcomes.

MAPI in IoT-Driven Business Environments

The convergence of Internet of Things (IoT) technologies with business communication systems has created new opportunities for automation, real-time decision-making, and operational efficiency. In this evolving landscape, MAPI, or Messaging Application Programming Interface, plays a critical role in enabling seamless integration between messaging platforms like Microsoft Exchange and the growing ecosystem of IoT devices. IoT-driven business environments rely on networks of connected sensors, devices, and machines that continuously generate data and trigger events. By leveraging MAPI, organizations can bridge the gap between machine-generated information and human-centric communication workflows, facilitating automated notifications, intelligent alerting, and streamlined collaboration across operational and managerial teams.

In modern industrial environments such as manufacturing, logistics, and utilities, IoT sensors and devices monitor equipment performance, environmental conditions, and process metrics in real-time. When anomalies are detected—such as temperature fluctuations in a cold storage unit, mechanical faults in production machinery, or network outages in remote facilities—automated systems need to relay this information swiftly to human operators and decision-makers. MAPI serves as a critical enabler of these workflows by providing the communication layer that allows IoT systems to send automated email alerts, schedule maintenance activities via calendar events, or distribute incident reports to relevant personnel through Microsoft Outlook or custom MAPI-enabled applications.

A common scenario involves IoT devices triggering maintenance workflows within smart factories. When a machine equipped with IoT sensors detects wear on critical components or deviates from predefined operational thresholds, the IoT system can generate an event that is processed by a backend automation platform. Through MAPI integration, this platform can create and send a detailed email notification directly to the maintenance team's shared mailbox, attaching diagnostic logs, sensor data, and recommended corrective actions. Additionally, the platform can use MAPI to automatically schedule a maintenance task in the team's Outlook calendars, ensuring the issue is addressed promptly while minimizing production downtime.

In supply chain and logistics environments, IoT devices installed in transport vehicles and warehouses continuously monitor factors such as shipment location, temperature, and humidity. Any deviation from optimal parameters can compromise the integrity of goods, especially in industries such as pharmaceuticals or food distribution. MAPI enables IoT systems to integrate with communication tools by automatically notifying supply chain managers when shipment conditions exceed acceptable thresholds. For instance, if an IoT sensor detects that a refrigerated shipment has exceeded safe temperature limits, the system can leverage MAPI to generate an urgent alert, distribute it to the logistics team, and escalate the incident by automatically scheduling a conference call with relevant stakeholders. This rapid information dissemination improves responsiveness and reduces the risk of product spoilage or regulatory non-compliance.

In the context of energy management and utilities, MAPI facilitates the integration of IoT-based monitoring solutions with operational communication workflows. Smart meters, grid sensors, and equipment monitoring systems generate alerts when service disruptions, load imbalances, or critical equipment failures occur. By using MAPI to create automated communication pipelines, energy companies can instantly relay outage notifications to field technicians, schedule inspection appointments on shared Outlook calendars, and keep customer service teams informed about service disruptions in specific regions. These automated MAPI-enabled workflows reduce the communication gap between field operations and customer-facing teams, enabling faster resolution times and improved customer satisfaction.

IoT devices are also widely used in facilities management, where building automation systems monitor HVAC performance, lighting, security systems, and occupancy data. When anomalies such as air conditioning failures or security breaches are detected, MAPI-integrated platforms can automatically notify facilities managers via email, generate incident tickets in helpdesk systems, and assign follow-up tasks through Outlook's task management features. For organizations managing large campuses or multi-location facilities, this automation ensures that facility-related issues are promptly communicated to the right teams and that corrective actions are scheduled efficiently.

Beyond operational notifications, MAPI can be integrated with IoT analytics platforms to support more strategic decision-making. IoT devices generate vast amounts of data that can reveal trends, inefficiencies, and opportunities for optimization. By combining MAPI with business intelligence tools, organizations can automate the generation of periodic reports that summarize IoT-derived insights. For example, a MAPI-enabled system could automatically email weekly reports on energy consumption trends, machine utilization rates, or environmental compliance metrics to department heads, complete with visualizations and actionable recommendations. This integration allows stakeholders to stay informed without manually retrieving data or generating reports.

Security and compliance are critical factors in IoT-driven business environments, where connected devices can become entry points for cyber threats. MAPI's role extends to automating security-related alerts triggered by IoT security platforms. When suspicious activity, such as unauthorized access attempts or firmware vulnerabilities, is detected by IoT security monitoring tools, MAPI can be used to immediately notify the IT security team via encrypted emails. The system can also leverage MAPI to initiate predefined incident response workflows, such as scheduling emergency meetings or sending action plans to incident response teams. This helps ensure that security threats are addressed promptly, reducing the potential impact on business operations.

In smart office environments, IoT devices that manage occupancy sensors, conference room availability, and resource utilization can integrate with MAPI to automate employee communication and resource booking. For instance, when occupancy sensors detect that a meeting room is vacant despite being booked, MAPI-enabled automation can release the booking and notify employees of the room's availability. Similarly, if resource usage trends suggest that specific office spaces are underutilized, facilities teams can receive automated reports via email to inform space reallocation decisions.

As IoT continues to grow in scale and complexity, the role of MAPI in supporting human-machine collaboration will become even more vital. The increasing adoption of edge computing in IoT ecosystems enables faster data processing closer to devices, and MAPI can serve as the bridge that ensures actionable insights are quickly disseminated to distributed teams. By integrating MAPI-based workflows with AI-powered IoT platforms, businesses can further enhance decision-making by automatically filtering and prioritizing alerts based on urgency and impact.

The value of MAPI in IoT-driven business environments lies in its ability to translate machine-generated data into actionable human communication through reliable, secure, and automated messaging workflows. Whether coordinating maintenance tasks, managing supply chain alerts, or streamlining energy management, MAPI provides the communication backbone that connects IoT ecosystems to enterprise collaboration tools like Outlook and Exchange. This integration not only improves operational efficiency but also empowers businesses to make faster, more informed decisions in real time, reinforcing the growing synergy between IoT and modern enterprise communication systems.

Developing Custom MAPI Solutions

Developing custom MAPI solutions allows businesses to extend and tailor their messaging workflows to meet unique operational needs. MAPI, or Messaging Application Programming Interface, is a powerful set of interfaces that enables applications to interact directly with messaging platforms such as Microsoft Exchange. While MAPI is most commonly associated with enabling client applications like Outlook to access email, calendars, tasks, and contacts, its full potential is unlocked when organizations develop custom solutions that automate processes, integrate with other business systems, and provide specialized functionality that off-the-shelf products may not offer.

Building custom MAPI solutions typically begins with identifying specific use cases where existing messaging workflows fall short or where additional automation can yield tangible efficiency gains. For example, businesses that manage high volumes of customer communications might require a system that automatically categorizes incoming emails, extracts relevant information, and integrates it with their CRM platform. A MAPI-based custom solution can monitor specific Exchange mailboxes, analyze message metadata and content, and then trigger downstream processes based on the data extracted. This allows customer service teams to reduce manual sorting and improve response times, ultimately enhancing customer satisfaction.

Developers building MAPI applications must work within the rich but complex MAPI framework, which provides access to a wide range of messaging objects and functions. Core components include message stores, folders, messages, attachments, recipients, and address books. By leveraging these components, custom solutions can manipulate messaging data with granular control. For instance, a legal firm might require an application that automatically scans incoming emails for contract documents, saves the attachments to a secure document management system, and logs the metadata—such as sender, subject, and timestamp—in a centralized database for audit and compliance purposes. With MAPI, developers can automate each step of this workflow, including reading attachments, creating records, and sending confirmation emails back to the sender.

One of the strengths of custom MAPI development lies in the ability to integrate messaging workflows with line-of-business applications. Organizations can create solutions that connect messaging data with ERP systems, project management platforms, or inventory management tools. For example, a manufacturing company could build a MAPI-enabled application that listens for order confirmation emails from suppliers. Upon receipt of an order confirmation, the system could extract order details from the email body or attachment and automatically update the ERP system to reflect pending deliveries. Simultaneously, the application could generate and send acknowledgment emails to internal procurement teams to confirm that inventory replenishment is underway.

Developing custom MAPI solutions also enables advanced automation of calendaring and scheduling processes. Many enterprises require highly coordinated meeting logistics, particularly when dealing with cross-functional teams, external partners, or executive stakeholders. A custom MAPI-based scheduling application can programmatically create Outlook calendar events, check attendee availability using the free/busy data available through MAPI, and send personalized invitations with pre-populated meeting details. In industries such as healthcare, where appointment scheduling is critical, MAPI solutions can automatically generate patient appointment emails, book time slots in medical practitioners' calendars, and issue reminders ahead of scheduled visits.

While MAPI offers powerful capabilities, developers must navigate its inherent complexity and adhere to best practices to ensure optimal performance. MAPI applications must manage session lifecycles efficiently, avoiding long-running connections that can lead to server resource contention. Careful handling of memory and object disposal is critical, as failing to release MAPI objects properly can result in memory leaks and degraded performance. Additionally, developers should batch-process messaging items where possible to minimize the number of server round trips, thereby reducing latency and improving scalability.

Security considerations are paramount when developing MAPI solutions, especially when handling sensitive messaging data. MAPI supports integration with Microsoft Exchange's built-in security features, including encryption of data in transit using SSL/TLS and the application of role-based access controls (RBAC). Custom applications should enforce user authentication using Active Directory credentials and limit data access based on the principle of least privilege. When building solutions that send or process external communications, developers should implement safeguards such as input validation, content filtering, and secure handling of attachments to mitigate risks related to data leakage, phishing, or malware propagation.

Another key area where custom MAPI solutions add value is in facilitating compliance with regulatory and corporate governance policies. Many industries require organizations to maintain comprehensive audit trails of messaging activities. Custom MAPI applications can automate the logging of email communications, track changes to public folders or shared mailboxes, and enforce retention policies by moving or archiving messages based on predefined rules. For example, a financial institution could develop a MAPI-based compliance tool that automatically flags and archives emails containing specific keywords, ensuring alignment with industry regulations such as GDPR, HIPAA, or SOX.

For businesses operating in hybrid environments, custom MAPI solutions must be designed to function across both on-premises Exchange servers and cloud-based Exchange Online mailboxes in Microsoft 365. This requires careful attention to authentication mechanisms, as hybrid environments often involve a mix of local Active Directory and Azure AD identities. Custom applications should support modern authentication protocols such as OAuth 2.0 to ensure secure access to cloud-hosted resources, while maintaining compatibility with legacy on-premises environments when necessary.

Testing and debugging are critical steps in the MAPI development lifecycle. Developers must thoroughly test applications under various network conditions and messaging loads to ensure reliability and performance. Logging mechanisms should be incorporated to capture diagnostic information, such as API call success rates, exception handling, and system resource usage. In production environments, these logs help administrators monitor application health, troubleshoot issues, and refine workflows based on observed patterns and user feedback.

Custom MAPI solutions also present opportunities to enhance user experience within client applications like Outlook. Developers can extend Outlook's functionality by creating custom add-ins or ribbons that integrate directly with MAPI-enabled workflows. For example, a sales team might benefit from a custom Outlook ribbon button that allows users to instantly categorize emails by client or project and push relevant data to the organization's CRM system without leaving their inbox. These user-centric enhancements improve adoption rates and ensure that business users can leverage automation with minimal disruption to their existing workflows.

Ultimately, developing custom MAPI solutions empowers organizations to build messaging workflows that are finely tuned to their business processes, industry requirements, and operational goals. By leveraging MAPI's full potential, businesses can automate repetitive tasks, integrate messaging data with critical business systems, enhance collaboration, and ensure that communication processes are efficient, secure, and aligned with enterprise-wide objectives. Skilled development teams, a deep understanding of MAPI's architecture, and a focus on scalability and security are essential to creating robust solutions that deliver lasting value in dynamic business environments.

API Gateways and MAPI Integration

As modern enterprises continue to embrace microservices architectures and cloud-native environments, API gateways have become a vital component in managing, securing, and scaling interactions between distributed systems. In parallel, MAPI, or Messaging Application Programming Interface, remains a cornerstone in enabling applications to interact with Microsoft Exchange servers for messaging services such as email, calendaring, contact management, and task automation. The integration of API gateways with MAPI-based services allows organizations to extend MAPI functionality beyond traditional on-premises applications, enabling secure and streamlined communication workflows across hybrid and multi-cloud environments. This integration represents a convergence of legacy messaging protocols with modern API-driven ecosystems, supporting business agility, enhanced security, and operational scalability.

API gateways function as centralized entry points for managing and routing API traffic between client applications and backend services. They provide capabilities such as request routing, load balancing, rate limiting, authentication, and logging, ensuring that API traffic is both optimized and secure. When integrated with MAPI-based systems, API gateways act as intermediaries that facilitate communication between business applications and MAPI-enabled services, such as Exchange servers. This architecture allows organizations to expose MAPI functionality—traditionally accessed via thick clients like Outlook or internal custom applications—through secure and standardized RESTful or SOAP APIs that external and modern cloud-native applications can consume.

One of the primary use cases for integrating API gateways with MAPI involves enabling modern web and mobile applications to leverage Exchange messaging services without directly interacting with the MAPI protocol. Since MAPI is a low-level, complex API traditionally used in Windows environments, exposing its capabilities through HTTP-based APIs simplifies integration for development teams building applications in diverse programming languages and frameworks. By deploying an API gateway to front-end a set of REST APIs that abstract common MAPI operations—such as sending emails, scheduling meetings, managing contacts, or retrieving mailbox contents—organizations create an integration layer that is easier to maintain, scale, and secure.

Security is a critical driver behind the adoption of API gateways in MAPI-enabled environments. API gateways support advanced security features such as OAuth 2.0, JWT (JSON Web Token) validation, and integration with identity providers like Azure Active Directory, ensuring that only authenticated and authorized clients can access MAPI-based services. This is especially important when exposing MAPI functionality to external applications or users over the internet. Instead of exposing the MAPI protocol directly, organizations can use the gateway to enforce granular access control policies, filter traffic based on IP allowlists or geolocation data, and apply rate limiting to prevent abuse or denial-of-service (DoS) attacks.

Another advantage of integrating MAPI with API gateways is the ability to standardize and simplify logging, monitoring, and analytics across communication workflows. API gateways capture detailed telemetry on all API requests and responses, including performance metrics, error rates, and usage patterns. When these metrics are aggregated with logs generated by MAPI-based systems, businesses gain a comprehensive view of messaging workflows, helping administrators identify bottlenecks, troubleshoot issues, and ensure compliance with regulatory or internal policies. For example, an organization could track metrics on how many automated emails were sent via MAPI through the API gateway in a given period, correlate this data with business KPIs, and identify opportunities for further workflow optimization.

Enterprises operating in hybrid environments—where Exchange servers are deployed both on-premises and in the cloud—benefit significantly from MAPI and API gateway integration. In hybrid models, MAPI workflows may need to span multiple infrastructures, including legacy data centers, Microsoft 365 services, and third-party cloud platforms. By positioning an API gateway at the intersection of these environments, organizations can facilitate secure, centralized access to MAPI-enabled services regardless of where Exchange servers or consuming applications are hosted. This centralized control plane enables businesses to seamlessly integrate MAPI with cloud-native applications running in Kubernetes clusters, SaaS platforms, or partner ecosystems while maintaining a consistent security and governance model.

The integration also supports automation and orchestration efforts within modern IT environments. API gateways allow MAPI functionality to be incorporated into automated CI/CD pipelines, workflow automation platforms, and robotic process automation (RPA) tools. For instance, a financial institution might use an API gateway to expose MAPI-based services that automatically send regulatory compliance reports via email on a scheduled basis, or trigger meeting invitations when certain operational thresholds are exceeded. Because the gateway abstracts the complexity of direct MAPI calls, development teams can focus on orchestrating these workflows through API-centric tools without needing specialized MAPI expertise.

In addition to traditional REST and SOAP protocols, some API gateways support GraphQL, enabling organizations to expose MAPI-powered data queries through flexible and efficient GraphQL APIs. This allows client applications to request exactly the data they need from Exchange environments, reducing payload sizes and improving performance in bandwidth-constrained or mobile environments. For example, a mobile sales enablement app could use GraphQL to fetch a list of unread emails and related calendar events for a user while filtering by specific project tags, without retrieving unnecessary data.

MAPI and API gateway integration is particularly valuable in industries with strict regulatory and compliance requirements. API gateways enable centralized enforcement of data protection policies, including automatic encryption of API payloads, content inspection, and request sanitization to prevent data leaks or injection attacks. Additionally, audit logs generated by the gateway provide a critical audit trail of all API interactions, supporting regulatory reporting and internal governance frameworks. This is essential for industries such as healthcare, finance, and government, where secure and compliant communication workflows are non-negotiable.

Performance optimization is another key benefit of using API gateways in conjunction with MAPI. Gateways offer built-in caching mechanisms to store frequent API responses, reducing the number of MAPI calls required to backend Exchange servers. For example, cached responses for directory lookups, address book queries, or frequently accessed mailbox metadata can improve application responsiveness while alleviating the load on messaging infrastructure. Load balancing and traffic shaping capabilities built into the API gateway further ensure that MAPI-based services remain resilient and performant under varying traffic conditions.

As organizations continue to modernize their technology stacks, the role of API gateways in integrating legacy systems like MAPI with contemporary applications will continue to grow. By bridging the gap between complex messaging protocols and API-driven business ecosystems, API gateways provide a scalable, secure, and efficient path for extending the value of MAPI-based services into the digital-first, cloud-centric world. Whether supporting automation, enhancing security, or driving integration across hybrid and multi-cloud infrastructures, the combination of MAPI and API gateways enables businesses to future-proof their messaging and collaboration environments while unlocking new efficiencies across the enterprise.

MAPI in the Context of Digital Transformation

Digital transformation is reshaping the way organizations approach operations, customer engagement, and internal collaboration. As businesses move toward more agile, data-driven models supported by cloud technologies, automation, and integrated communication ecosystems, legacy protocols like MAPI, or Messaging Application Programming Interface, remain highly relevant. MAPI continues to play a foundational role in enabling the seamless flow of information within modern enterprises. Its presence in critical communication workflows, especially in environments powered by Microsoft Exchange and Outlook, provides a stable platform on which businesses can build their digital transformation initiatives.

In the context of digital transformation, organizations aim to automate manual processes, integrate disparate systems, and enhance the speed and accuracy of decision-making. MAPI supports these objectives by serving as the bridge between business applications and the enterprise messaging infrastructure. While many digital transformation efforts focus on adopting cutting-edge technologies like artificial intelligence, machine learning, and cloud-native applications, the importance of reliable communication protocols such as MAPI cannot be overlooked. MAPI facilitates the automation of critical processes such as scheduling, notification delivery, and document workflows, ensuring that communication remains integrated and secure across enterprise systems.

A significant aspect of digital transformation is the migration of traditional workloads to the cloud. Many organizations are shifting from on-premises Exchange servers to Exchange Online as part of Microsoft 365, adopting hybrid or fully cloud-based models. MAPI's evolution, including the introduction of MAPI over HTTP, ensures compatibility with both legacy systems and modern cloud infrastructures. This backward compatibility and forward scalability make MAPI a critical enabler of hybrid communication environments. Enterprises benefit from maintaining consistent communication protocols across both cloud-hosted and on-premises mailboxes, ensuring users experience a unified interface and consistent access to messaging services regardless of where their data resides.

Automation is at the heart of digital transformation, and MAPI plays a key role in this domain by enabling the automation of communication-based workflows. Businesses increasingly integrate MAPI with ERP systems, CRM platforms, and custom applications to automate repetitive messaging tasks. For example, an organization may develop a solution that leverages MAPI to automate order confirmations by pulling transaction data from its ERP system and sending templated emails to customers via Exchange. MAPI can also automate internal workflows, such as sending project milestone reminders to teams or automatically creating meeting invitations based on business process triggers. These integrations eliminate manual steps, reduce human error, and speed up the completion of critical tasks.

Another crucial component of digital transformation is enhancing customer engagement through personalized and timely communication. MAPI supports this by allowing businesses to automate and customize email campaigns based on customer behavior or transaction history. For instance, a retail company can use MAPI-integrated systems to automatically send promotional offers, invoices, or account updates directly from its backend systems, creating seamless and timely touchpoints with customers. The ability to personalize communication through MAPI's fine-grained control over message headers, body content, and attachments helps businesses deliver a more engaging and relevant customer experience.

MAPI also plays a significant role in integrating communication workflows with collaboration platforms. As organizations adopt tools like Microsoft Teams and SharePoint to support modern workplace initiatives, MAPI ensures that email, calendar, and task data remains synchronized with these platforms. Automated workflows powered by MAPI can bridge the gap between formal email communications and real-time collaboration channels. For example, when a critical project update is received via email, a MAPI-based integration can automatically post relevant details to a Microsoft Teams channel, ensuring that project stakeholders are immediately informed and can collaborate in real time. This cross-platform integration streamlines communication and fosters faster decision-making, both of which are essential goals of digital transformation efforts.

Security and compliance considerations are at the core of any digital transformation initiative, particularly as businesses handle increasing volumes of sensitive data across complex ecosystems. MAPI enables organizations to implement secure communication workflows that comply with data protection regulations such as GDPR, HIPAA, or SOX. By integrating MAPI with Microsoft Exchange security features, businesses can enforce email encryption, apply sensitivity labels, and automate the archiving of critical communications in compliance with regulatory mandates. Additionally, MAPI allows for the creation of custom solutions that monitor and log communication activity, providing the transparency and auditability required by modern governance frameworks.

Digital transformation also demands real-time access to data and analytics, and MAPI supports this by enabling business systems to interact dynamically with messaging data. By integrating MAPI with analytics platforms, organizations can capture valuable insights from email traffic, calendar usage patterns, and task management trends. These insights can inform operational improvements, identify communication bottlenecks, and highlight opportunities for further process automation. For instance, analyzing meeting frequency and scheduling conflicts through MAPI data can lead to optimized resource planning and improved employee productivity.

One of the key advantages of MAPI in digital transformation is its extensibility. Organizations can develop custom MAPI-enabled applications or services tailored to their unique business requirements. Whether building custom Outlook add-ins to streamline document approval workflows or integrating MAPI with AI-driven virtual assistants for automated meeting scheduling, businesses can extend their communication capabilities while aligning with broader digital transformation goals. MAPI serves as a flexible integration layer that allows enterprises to modernize communication workflows without completely overhauling existing infrastructure.

As digital transformation accelerates the adoption of hybrid work models, MAPI ensures that remote and distributed teams have consistent and secure access to enterprise messaging systems. Employees working from remote locations rely on MAPI to access shared calendars, public folders, and corporate email systems through Outlook or custom applications, ensuring business continuity and operational resilience. MAPI over HTTP further enhances this capability by providing a modern, secure transport protocol that performs reliably across various network conditions, supporting the fluidity required by remote and hybrid workforces.

The role of MAPI in digital transformation extends to supporting enterprise-wide initiatives such as business continuity and disaster recovery. By automating the delivery of critical incident notifications, backup reports, and continuity plans through MAPI-integrated workflows, businesses can ensure that essential communications are disseminated efficiently during emergencies. Furthermore, MAPI's compatibility with on-premises, hybrid, and cloud infrastructures enables organizations to implement resilient communication strategies that safeguard business operations against disruptions.

Ultimately, MAPI's place in digital transformation is defined by its ability to bridge traditional messaging protocols with modern business ecosystems. As organizations embrace cloud computing, automation, and data-driven decision-making, MAPI continues to serve as a vital enabler of integrated communication workflows. Its capacity to support hybrid models, facilitate secure and automated messaging, and integrate with diverse business applications positions MAPI as a key component of the modern enterprise's digital transformation journey. Through MAPI, businesses can modernize their operations, accelerate innovation, and deliver enhanced value to customers and stakeholders in an increasingly connected and dynamic world.

Reducing Operational Costs with MAPI

Organizations today are under constant pressure to reduce operational costs while maintaining or improving the quality of their internal and external communications. MAPI, or Messaging Application Programming Interface, has long been associated with facilitating seamless communication between client applications and messaging servers such as Microsoft Exchange. However, beyond its technical capabilities, MAPI serves as a strategic tool for driving cost efficiency across a wide variety of business processes. By automating tasks, streamlining workflows, reducing manual intervention, and optimizing resource usage, MAPI enables organizations to lower operational expenditures while enhancing productivity.

One of the primary ways MAPI contributes to cost reduction is through workflow automation. Many businesses still rely on manual processes to handle repetitive communication tasks such as routing emails, scheduling meetings, or distributing reports. These manual efforts consume valuable employee time, which could otherwise be directed toward higher-value activities. With MAPI, organizations can automate routine messaging workflows across departments. For example, a finance team can automate the generation and emailing of monthly financial reports, eliminating the need for staff to manually compile, format, and distribute documents. Similarly, HR departments can use MAPI to automatically schedule interviews, send onboarding materials, or generate personalized notifications for employee milestones. The cumulative effect of such automation leads to significant labor cost savings across the enterprise.

MAPI also plays a role in reducing IT maintenance and support costs by simplifying client-server communication. By standardizing on MAPI over HTTP, organizations ensure more stable and secure connectivity between Outlook clients and Exchange servers. This minimizes the frequency of connection errors, synchronization issues, and user-reported incidents related to messaging services. Fewer support tickets translate to a reduced workload for IT helpdesk teams, which means organizations can reallocate IT resources to more strategic initiatives. Furthermore, MAPI-enabled environments require less frequent troubleshooting of legacy protocols such as RPC over HTTP, further reducing time and expenses associated with legacy system maintenance.

The optimization of resource utilization is another avenue where MAPI generates cost savings. In large enterprises, inefficient handling of messaging resources can result in server overload, unnecessary hardware expenditures, or wasted storage capacity. MAPI provides organizations with granular control over how messaging data is accessed, manipulated, and stored. For instance, through MAPI-integrated workflows, IT teams can implement retention policies that automatically archive or delete outdated emails, reducing the storage footprint on costly mail servers and cloud storage subscriptions. In addition, organizations can automate mailbox size monitoring and trigger corrective actions, such as alerting users to clean up oversized mailboxes, without manual oversight. These measures help optimize server performance and delay the need for infrastructure upgrades.

MAPI also supports operational cost reduction through enhanced integration with existing business applications. By using MAPI to connect messaging systems with ERP, CRM, and project management tools, organizations can eliminate the need for third-party middleware or complex custom-built integrations. For example, a sales team might rely on a CRM platform that automatically logs email communications with clients via MAPI integration, reducing the need for manual data entry and minimizing errors. Avoiding the licensing and maintenance costs associated with additional integration platforms helps businesses streamline their technology stack while improving overall operational efficiency.

Remote work and hybrid work models have become integral to modern business operations, and MAPI plays a pivotal role in reducing costs associated with supporting distributed workforces. With MAPI over HTTP, remote employees can securely access Exchange-based services from any location without the need for expensive VPN infrastructure or dedicated remote access solutions. This capability reduces the overhead associated with maintaining remote connectivity tools and improves end-user productivity by providing direct, reliable access to corporate email, calendars, and task lists via Outlook or custom MAPI-based applications. Additionally, IT teams can automate profile configuration and mailbox setup for remote workers, further reducing onboarding costs and accelerating time to productivity.

MAPI enhances operational efficiency by enabling centralized administration of communication workflows. Administrators can deploy MAPI-enabled scripts and automation tools to manage mailboxes, apply security policies, configure permissions, and execute bulk operations without the need for manual intervention. These automated administrative processes reduce the dependency on large IT teams to handle day-to-day messaging system management. For example, MAPI-based automation can simplify the onboarding and offboarding process by automatically provisioning or decommissioning user mailboxes, applying access controls, and archiving data according to company policy, reducing both labor costs and the risk of human error.

Reducing compliance-related costs is another key benefit of MAPI implementation. In regulated industries, organizations must adhere to strict data protection, retention, and auditing requirements. MAPI supports compliance efforts by enabling the automation of email classification, encryption, and archiving workflows. Instead of relying on manual processes to enforce data protection policies, businesses can use MAPI to automatically apply sensitivity labels to emails based on their content or recipients, ensuring compliance with standards such as GDPR, HIPAA, or SOX. This automation reduces the burden on compliance teams and mitigates the risk of regulatory fines, legal fees, and reputational damage resulting from non-compliance.

Moreover, MAPI supports integration with monitoring and analytics tools that help organizations identify cost-saving opportunities. By collecting data on messaging traffic patterns, resource utilization, and user behavior, businesses can uncover inefficiencies in communication workflows. For instance, analytics might reveal that certain departments generate an excessive volume of redundant emails or that underutilized public folders are consuming significant storage resources. MAPI-integrated insights allow organizations to take corrective action, such as optimizing email distribution lists, consolidating shared mailboxes, or adjusting policies to reduce storage and bandwidth consumption.

Another important aspect of cost reduction through MAPI is the enablement of self-service capabilities for end-users. By integrating MAPI with custom applications or Outlook add-ins, businesses can empower employees to complete routine tasks without IT intervention. For example, an Outlook add-in could allow employees to request distribution list changes, report mailbox issues, or schedule recurring team meetings directly within the Outlook interface. Reducing the volume of requests submitted to IT support teams lowers operational overhead and shortens resolution times.

Finally, by extending MAPI's capabilities to support mobile devices and external applications, organizations reduce the need for redundant communication tools. Instead of investing in multiple messaging systems for desktop, web, and mobile platforms, businesses can rely on a single, MAPI-enabled messaging ecosystem that serves all endpoints. This consolidation reduces software licensing costs, simplifies user training, and ensures consistency across communication channels.

In summary, MAPI's role in reducing operational costs is multifaceted. Through workflow automation, improved resource utilization, secure remote access, centralized administration, and seamless integration with business systems, MAPI helps organizations streamline operations while lowering the expenses associated with communication infrastructure and labor. As businesses continue to prioritize efficiency and cost control, MAPI will remain a valuable component in achieving these objectives within modern, hybrid IT environments.

MAPI and Business Intelligence Tools

The integration of MAPI, or Messaging Application Programming Interface, with business intelligence (BI) tools presents a powerful opportunity for organizations to extract valuable insights from their messaging systems. MAPI serves as the core interface enabling client applications and custom solutions to interact with Microsoft Exchange servers, accessing and managing emails, calendars, contacts, and other messaging objects. By leveraging MAPI's capabilities, businesses can unlock detailed operational data from their messaging workflows and connect this information with BI platforms to support data-driven decision-making. As businesses increasingly seek to optimize communication, improve productivity, and align operations with strategic goals, combining MAPI with BI tools has become a crucial element of modern enterprise analytics.

MAPI acts as a conduit for accessing rich datasets stored within an organization's Exchange environment. These datasets include metadata such as message timestamps, sender and recipient details, email subjects, message body content, attachment information, and calendar event properties. When integrated with BI tools, this information can be aggregated, processed, and visualized to reveal trends, inefficiencies, and opportunities for improvement across the organization. For example, a business can use MAPI to extract data related to internal email traffic patterns, identifying departments with unusually high communication volumes, bottlenecks in project workflows, or silos that hinder collaboration. This granular visibility into communication habits helps organizations make informed decisions about restructuring teams, reallocating resources, or implementing policies to encourage more efficient collaboration.

MAPI enables businesses to extend business intelligence beyond traditional operational and financial metrics by providing insights into communication behaviors and interactions. By integrating MAPI with platforms such as Microsoft Power BI, Tableau, or Qlik, organizations can create dashboards that display key performance indicators (KPIs) related to messaging workflows. For example, visualizations might include average response times to client emails, frequency of follow-up communications, volume of unread messages by team or department, or calendar utilization rates across different business units. These metrics offer a deeper understanding of how internal and external communication flows affect productivity, customer satisfaction, and project delivery timelines.

In customer service environments, integrating MAPI with BI tools enables businesses to track and analyze customer interactions more effectively. When customer support teams rely on shared mailboxes or distribution lists to handle client inquiries, MAPI can be used to extract data on response times, escalation rates, and issue resolution trends. BI dashboards powered by this data help managers identify patterns such as recurring customer complaints, peak periods of customer inquiries, or underperformance within certain teams. With this information, organizations can implement targeted training programs, optimize staffing levels, or adjust service-level agreements to enhance customer satisfaction and operational efficiency.

Sales and marketing teams also benefit from MAPI and BI integration. By pulling data on outbound communication campaigns, lead follow-ups, and client meeting schedules, businesses can measure the effectiveness of sales strategies and marketing outreach efforts. MAPI enables the extraction of data on email open rates, attachment downloads, and meeting acceptance rates when combined with custom tracking mechanisms or CRM integrations. When visualized through BI platforms, these insights allow sales leaders to identify which tactics generate the highest engagement and revenue opportunities, allowing them to refine sales processes and improve campaign targeting.

Another critical advantage of integrating MAPI with business intelligence tools is in resource management and capacity planning. By analyzing calendar data accessed via MAPI, organizations can track meeting frequency, scheduling conflicts, and room booking patterns across departments or office locations. Facilities managers can use this data to optimize the allocation of meeting spaces, invest in additional collaboration resources, or adjust policies related to recurring meetings and room reservations. Similarly, project managers can review team calendars to identify potential scheduling bottlenecks or resource shortages that could impact project timelines.

Compliance and governance are additional areas where MAPI and BI integration offer significant value. Many organizations must adhere to strict regulatory requirements concerning data retention, auditability, and communication monitoring. MAPI provides direct access to message metadata and mailbox audit logs, which can be processed by BI tools to ensure adherence to internal policies and regulatory standards. For example, compliance officers can use BI dashboards to track instances where sensitive data was shared externally, monitor mailbox access by privileged users, or ensure that emails are archived and retained according to company policies. This level of visibility reduces the risk of regulatory non-compliance, financial penalties, or reputational damage.

MAPI also supports advanced analytics by enabling sentiment analysis and content categorization through integration with AI-driven BI platforms. When paired with natural language processing (NLP) models, MAPI can be used to extract and analyze the content of emails and meeting notes, identifying sentiment trends within customer communications or employee interactions. This insight allows businesses to address negative sentiment before it escalates, optimize customer service processes, and foster a more collaborative internal environment. For instance, a customer experience team might use sentiment analysis dashboards to identify clients expressing dissatisfaction across multiple channels and proactively reach out to resolve concerns.

The integration of MAPI with business intelligence tools is not limited to historical reporting; it also supports real-time alerting and proactive decision-making. Organizations can implement MAPI-enabled monitoring systems that trigger alerts when specific thresholds are met. For example, if an unusually high volume of urgent emails is detected in a shared incident management mailbox, the system can generate an alert and visualize the incident on a live dashboard. This immediate visibility empowers teams to respond quickly to critical situations, improving crisis management capabilities and reducing response times.

For organizations operating in hybrid environments, combining MAPI with BI tools helps unify insights across on-premises and cloud-hosted messaging infrastructures. As businesses adopt Exchange Online or hybrid Exchange configurations, MAPI ensures that communication data is consistently available for analysis, regardless of where mailboxes are hosted. BI platforms can consolidate this data into comprehensive enterprise-wide dashboards, providing leadership with a holistic view of communication trends and their impact on business performance.

Developing a successful MAPI and BI integration strategy requires careful planning and attention to data governance, scalability, and security. Businesses must ensure that messaging data is extracted, transformed, and loaded into BI tools securely and efficiently. Sensitive data must be protected during transmission and processing, with access controls in place to limit who can view or manipulate communication datasets. MAPI's compatibility with security protocols such as SSL/TLS and Exchange's role-based access controls helps ensure that integration projects comply with industry best practices and regulatory requirements.

Ultimately, combining MAPI with business intelligence tools provides organizations with actionable insights that extend far beyond traditional email and calendar functions. By harnessing the full potential of their messaging data, businesses can drive operational improvements, enhance employee productivity, improve customer satisfaction, and align communication workflows with broader strategic goals. MAPI's versatility and deep integration with Exchange environments make it an indispensable enabler of data-driven decision-making in modern enterprises.

The Role of MAPI in Supply Chain Communication

In today's globalized and highly interconnected business environment, supply chain operations depend on precise and timely communication between manufacturers, suppliers, distributors, logistics providers, and end customers. The seamless flow of information across all these stakeholders ensures the efficiency, agility, and resilience of supply chains. MAPI, or Messaging Application Programming Interface, plays a vital role in facilitating this communication by integrating business applications and automating workflows through secure and structured messaging systems. By enabling enterprises to automate supply chain-related emails, calendar events, and document management tasks, MAPI helps improve collaboration, reduce delays, and enhance overall supply chain performance.

One of the most significant contributions of MAPI to supply chain communication is the automation of transactional messaging between organizations and their suppliers or logistics partners. Orders, shipment confirmations, invoices, and delivery notices traditionally rely on email as a primary communication channel. Through MAPI, businesses can integrate their ERP or inventory management systems directly with their Microsoft Exchange servers, enabling the automatic generation and delivery of these messages. For example, when a purchase order is created in the ERP system, MAPI can trigger an automated email to the supplier containing the order details, delivery timelines, and payment terms. This reduces the need for manual data entry and eliminates delays caused by human oversight or bottlenecks in the approval chain.

Additionally, MAPI supports the automatic processing and routing of inbound emails within supply chain workflows. When suppliers send order confirmations, invoices, or shipping updates, MAPI-enabled applications can automatically monitor designated mailboxes and process incoming messages according to predefined business rules. For instance, an automated MAPI-based workflow could read the contents of an email from a logistics provider, extract shipment tracking information from the attached documents, and update the shipment status in the organization's supply chain management platform. At the same time, the system could automatically route the email to the relevant purchasing or warehouse teams, ensuring they have real-time visibility into the progress of the delivery.

MAPI also enhances communication efficiency through calendar automation and meeting coordination. Supply chain operations often require frequent coordination between cross-functional teams, such as production planning, procurement, logistics, and customer service. MAPI allows business applications to programmatically schedule and manage meetings based on real-time supply chain events. For example, if a critical shipment delay is detected, a MAPI-enabled system could automatically create and send calendar invitations for a virtual meeting between procurement managers, logistics providers, and customer service representatives to address the issue and adjust timelines. This reduces the lag time in coordinating responses to supply chain disruptions and improves collaboration across geographically dispersed teams.

Another important role of MAPI in supply chain communication is its ability to integrate with document management systems. Supply chains generate large volumes of essential documents such as bills of lading, packing lists, certificates of origin, and customs declarations. By integrating MAPI with document management platforms like SharePoint, businesses can automate the archiving and categorization of such documents. For instance, when a shipping confirmation email is received, MAPI can be used to extract the relevant attachments and automatically store them in a centralized document repository. The system can tag the documents with metadata such as supplier name, shipment date, and order number, making them easy to retrieve during audits or compliance reviews.

In environments where supply chains operate on just-in-time principles, speed and accuracy of communication are paramount. MAPI contributes to reducing lead times and mitigating risks associated with stockouts or production halts by facilitating faster and more reliable messaging workflows. Automated alert systems built on MAPI can notify supply chain managers when inventory levels fall below critical thresholds or when disruptions occur within the supplier network. These alerts can be configured to include actionable information such as supplier contact details, alternative vendor recommendations, or escalation procedures, enabling decision-makers to respond quickly and effectively.

The role of MAPI extends to enhancing customer-facing communication within the supply chain ecosystem. When orders are fulfilled and shipments are dispatched, MAPI can automate the generation of delivery notifications to end customers, providing them with shipment tracking information and estimated delivery times. This improves customer satisfaction by offering greater transparency and minimizing the volume of customer service inquiries related to order status. Additionally, MAPI enables businesses to automate post-delivery communication, such as customer feedback requests or warranty registration emails, helping organizations maintain a positive relationship with their customers after the fulfillment process.

MAPI also contributes to supply chain resilience by supporting the development of contingency workflows during disruptions. In cases where unexpected events such as natural disasters, transportation strikes, or geopolitical instability impact supply chain operations, MAPI-enabled systems can automate the notification process across the organization. Procurement teams, logistics providers, and executive leadership can receive automated updates on the status of affected shipments, and emergency response teams can be mobilized by automatically scheduling crisis management meetings. This level of automation reduces the time needed to implement contingency plans and helps minimize the financial and reputational impact of supply chain disruptions.

In industries where regulatory compliance is a key concern, MAPI supports supply chain communication by enforcing secure messaging practices. Organizations that transport sensitive or regulated goods, such as pharmaceuticals, chemicals, or electronics, must adhere to strict documentation and communication standards. MAPI can be integrated with security solutions such as S/MIME to ensure that sensitive supply chain emails are encrypted and digitally signed, protecting data integrity and confidentiality. Additionally, MAPI workflows can automatically classify and archive regulated communications, ensuring that document retention policies are consistently enforced and that records are readily available during audits or inspections.

Finally, the ability of MAPI to integrate with business intelligence and analytics platforms provides supply chain leaders with greater visibility into communication performance. By analyzing messaging patterns, response times, and communication volumes using MAPI-extracted data, businesses can identify areas where supply chain communication can be improved. For instance, if analysis reveals that certain suppliers consistently delay order confirmations, procurement managers can take proactive steps to address these inefficiencies, renegotiate terms, or identify alternative suppliers. These data-driven insights enable organizations to continuously improve supply chain performance and reduce risks associated with communication breakdowns.

MAPI's role in supply chain communication is multifaceted, providing critical automation, integration, and security capabilities that enable enterprises to operate more efficiently and effectively. Whether managing complex supplier networks, coordinating logistics workflows, or enhancing customer communication, MAPI serves as a key enabler of streamlined, responsive, and resilient supply chain operations. As supply chains continue to evolve and become more digitally integrated, the importance of tools like MAPI in maintaining smooth and transparent communication across all stages of the value chain will only continue to grow.

Improving Customer Experience Through MAPI

In today's highly competitive business landscape, customer experience is one of the key differentiators that sets successful organizations apart. Customers expect timely responses, personalized interactions, and seamless service across every touchpoint. MAPI, or Messaging Application Programming Interface, plays a significant role in helping businesses deliver superior customer experiences by enabling integrated and automated communication workflows. While traditionally viewed as the backbone for Outlook and Exchange communications, MAPI's capabilities extend far beyond simple email delivery, directly influencing how businesses engage with customers at scale.

At the core of customer experience is the ability to provide timely and relevant communication. MAPI enables organizations to automate customer interactions by integrating communication workflows directly with back-end business systems such as CRM platforms, helpdesk solutions, and customer portals. For instance, when a customer places an order or submits a service request, MAPI-based applications can automatically generate personalized confirmation emails containing order details, estimated delivery times, or ticket numbers. These communications not only reassure customers that their request has been received but also create transparency that fosters trust. Automating these touchpoints reduces manual intervention, minimizes the risk of delays, and ensures that customers consistently receive accurate information.

Personalization is another critical element of customer experience, and MAPI provides organizations with the tools to tailor communication based on individual customer profiles. By leveraging customer data stored within integrated CRM systems, MAPI-enabled workflows can dynamically populate outgoing messages with customer-specific information such as purchase history, preferences, or loyalty program details. For example, a MAPI-based solution could automatically send targeted promotional offers or personalized recommendations via email, increasing customer engagement and improving conversion rates. These customized interactions help customers feel valued and understood, which is a cornerstone of building long-term relationships and brand loyalty.

MAPI also enhances the responsiveness of customer service teams by automating the routing and prioritization of incoming messages. Customer inquiries often arrive through shared mailboxes or generic service addresses. MAPI can be used to develop intelligent systems that monitor these mailboxes and automatically categorize messages based on content, sentiment, or urgency. For instance, messages containing keywords such as complaint or refund can be flagged as high-priority and routed to senior support agents, while general inquiries are assigned to the appropriate team. By ensuring that critical customer issues are addressed swiftly, organizations can reduce resolution times and demonstrate a commitment to customer satisfaction.

Beyond email automation, MAPI plays a pivotal role in improving appointment scheduling and service coordination. For businesses that operate in industries such as healthcare, consulting, or field services, efficient scheduling is essential to a positive customer experience. MAPI enables organizations to integrate appointment booking systems directly with Outlook calendars. Customers can receive automated booking confirmations, appointment reminders, or rescheduling notices without manual involvement from service teams. Additionally, MAPI allows customer-facing teams to access real-time availability data, reducing the chances of double-booking or missed appointments. This level of convenience and professionalism helps create a smoother and more reliable customer journey.

MAPI further supports post-interaction engagement, an often-overlooked aspect of customer experience. Following a service appointment, product delivery, or support resolution, businesses can use MAPI-based workflows to automate follow-up communications. For example, an organization can automatically send satisfaction surveys, thank-you notes, or upsell offers based on recent customer interactions. These follow-ups show that the business values customer feedback and is invested in continuous improvement. Additionally, collecting feedback through automated workflows allows businesses to gather actionable insights that can be used to enhance future customer interactions.

Another way MAPI improves customer experience is by facilitating seamless cross-departmental collaboration. When customer cases require input from multiple teams, such as technical support, billing, or legal, MAPI enables organizations to automate internal notifications and ensure that all stakeholders have visibility into the customer's case. A MAPI-based system might automatically generate calendar invitations for cross-functional meetings, share customer correspondence across departments, or update shared mailboxes with the latest case notes. By streamlining internal communication, businesses can resolve customer issues more efficiently and present a unified front to the customer.

Security and compliance are increasingly important to customers who entrust businesses with their personal information. MAPI supports secure communication practices by enabling organizations to apply encryption, digital signatures, and sensitivity labels to customer communications. For example, businesses handling sensitive data such as financial statements, medical records, or legal contracts can use MAPI to ensure that emails are securely transmitted and protected against unauthorized access. By proactively safeguarding customer data, organizations can build trust and demonstrate their commitment to protecting customer interests.

MAPI's role extends to improving customer self-service capabilities. By integrating MAPI with customer portals or chatbot platforms, businesses can automate the distribution of key account information, support articles, or personalized content via email. When a customer requests a password reset, account statement, or technical documentation, MAPI-based workflows can automatically generate and send the requested information without requiring human intervention. Enabling customers to resolve common issues quickly and independently contributes to a frictionless experience that meets modern expectations for convenience and efficiency.

For organizations with global customer bases, MAPI helps ensure consistent and localized communication. MAPI-based applications can automate the delivery of communications in the customer's preferred language, adjusting time zones for appointment reminders or tailoring content to region-specific requirements. For instance, when launching a global marketing campaign, businesses can use MAPI to segment audiences by location and ensure that each customer receives regionally relevant messaging. This attention to localization improves engagement and reinforces the brand's reputation as customer-centric and culturally aware.

Finally, MAPI's integration with business intelligence tools enables organizations to continuously refine their customer experience strategies. By analyzing data extracted from customer communications—such as response times, interaction frequency, and sentiment—businesses can identify patterns and areas for improvement. For example, if analysis reveals that certain types of inquiries consistently experience delayed responses, customer service workflows can be restructured to prioritize those cases. MAPI's ability to facilitate this level of insight equips businesses with the data they need to deliver exceptional customer experiences at every stage of the customer lifecycle.

The role of MAPI in improving customer experience is deeply rooted in its ability to automate, personalize, and secure communication processes across the organization. By embedding MAPI-enabled workflows into core business systems, companies can eliminate friction in customer interactions, enhance responsiveness, and foster stronger relationships with their clients. As customer expectations continue to rise, businesses that leverage the full potential of MAPI will be better positioned to deliver consistent, high-quality service that drives customer satisfaction and long-term loyalty.

MAPI and Business Continuity Planning

Business continuity planning is a fundamental component of risk management, ensuring that critical operations can continue or be quickly restored in the event of unexpected disruptions. As modern organizations rely heavily on communication infrastructures to support day-to-day operations, client engagement, and collaboration across teams, the role of messaging systems in business continuity cannot be overstated. MAPI, or Messaging Application Programming Interface, is a key enabler in this context, as it facilitates the integration of communication workflows with Microsoft Exchange environments. By embedding MAPI into continuity plans, businesses ensure that essential communication channels remain operational, resilient, and secure, even when facing system failures, natural disasters, or cybersecurity incidents.

MAPI's primary function of enabling seamless interactions between messaging clients such as Outlook and Exchange servers makes it indispensable in environments where email and calendar services are mission-critical. Business continuity plans must address the continuity of MAPI-enabled messaging workflows, which are responsible for managing internal and external communications, scheduling, and task coordination. When an incident disrupts normal IT operations, such as a server crash, data center outage, or cyberattack, organizations must be able to rely on MAPI-based systems to maintain communication between employees, partners, and customers. This continuity helps minimize downtime, preserve client relationships, and prevent the escalation of operational challenges.

One of the key ways MAPI contributes to business continuity is through its support for high-availability configurations, such as Exchange Database Availability Groups (DAGs). MAPI-enabled clients automatically connect to active mailbox databases, even if a failover event occurs within the Exchange infrastructure. This resilience is critical in disaster scenarios, where primary data centers might go offline or individual Exchange servers become unavailable. MAPI ensures that Outlook clients and custom applications reconnect to healthy servers, maintaining uninterrupted access to mailboxes, calendars, and tasks. The ability of MAPI to work seamlessly across DAG failover processes is essential for businesses that require consistent communication capabilities under adverse conditions.

MAPI also plays a role in hybrid business continuity strategies. Many organizations have adopted hybrid messaging environments, where on-premises Exchange servers coexist with Exchange Online mailboxes in Microsoft 365. MAPI over HTTP supports secure and reliable communication across both infrastructures, allowing businesses to design continuity plans that leverage both local and cloud-based resources. In the event of a disaster affecting on-premises infrastructure, users can be temporarily redirected to cloud-hosted mailboxes, ensuring communication continuity without significant service degradation. This hybrid resilience empowers organizations to maintain critical workflows even when segments of their IT landscape are compromised.

Automation of incident response communications is another key advantage of MAPI in business continuity planning. When an unexpected disruption occurs, MAPI-based systems can automatically generate and distribute incident alerts, status updates, and recovery instructions to predefined distribution lists or emergency response teams. For example, a MAPI-enabled application can monitor key infrastructure components and trigger automated notifications when service thresholds are breached or when security incidents are detected. These notifications can include essential information such as the nature of the incident, initial impact assessment, and next steps, helping businesses mobilize response teams more quickly and reduce confusion during crisis scenarios.

In situations where immediate coordination is required, MAPI enables organizations to automate the scheduling of emergency meetings, both virtually and in person. By programmatically creating Outlook calendar events, MAPI-based systems can schedule cross-functional team meetings, allocate conference rooms, and send out meeting invites with detailed agendas. This capability ensures that crisis management teams can rapidly convene and implement recovery strategies without the delays associated with manual scheduling processes. For globally distributed organizations, MAPI's integration with time zone-aware scheduling features further enhances the efficiency of emergency coordination.

Maintaining secure communication channels during business disruptions is a core requirement of any continuity plan, and MAPI provides native support for encryption protocols such as SSL/TLS and S/MIME. When business continuity plans are activated, sensitive communications regarding business impact, legal considerations, or customer notifications must remain protected. MAPI facilitates this by ensuring that all communication between client applications and Exchange servers remains encrypted, reducing the risk of data interception or unauthorized access during a period of heightened vulnerability. Additionally, MAPI can integrate with data loss prevention (DLP) systems and apply automated sensitivity labeling to messages, further strengthening data protection efforts.

Business continuity planning also involves the maintenance of critical communication records for audit, legal, and compliance purposes. MAPI enables the automatic archiving of incident-related messages, ensuring that all communications sent and received during a business disruption are securely stored and easily retrievable. This archival process supports post-incident reviews, regulatory reporting, and internal governance requirements. By automating the logging of communication activities, organizations ensure full visibility into how information was shared and decisions were made during critical incidents.

Another important aspect of MAPI in business continuity is its ability to support remote and mobile workers. When access to physical offices or corporate networks is restricted due to environmental hazards, health emergencies, or other crises, MAPI over HTTP ensures that remote employees can continue to access Exchange-based communication services from their Outlook clients without relying on legacy VPN infrastructure. This direct, secure connection allows employees to send and receive emails, schedule meetings, and collaborate on tasks, helping maintain operational continuity and employee productivity during disruptions.

Integration with business intelligence and monitoring tools further enhances MAPI's role in continuity planning. By feeding MAPI-related performance data into centralized monitoring systems, businesses can detect anomalies in communication workflows, such as sudden drops in message delivery rates or unusual login patterns that may indicate service degradation or security breaches. Early detection enables IT teams to activate continuity protocols more quickly, minimizing the scope and impact of disruptions.

Additionally, MAPI can be embedded into tabletop exercises and business continuity drills to simulate real-world incident scenarios. During these exercises, organizations can test the ability of MAPI-enabled systems to send automated notifications, manage failover processes, and coordinate emergency meetings. These tests ensure that employees are familiar with the workflows and that any gaps in the continuity plan are identified and addressed before an actual incident occurs.

The role of MAPI in business continuity planning is further amplified in sectors such as finance, healthcare, and government, where regulatory frameworks demand continuous availability of critical communication services. By integrating MAPI into business continuity strategies, organizations in these sectors can meet uptime requirements, support compliance with regulations such as GDPR, HIPAA, and SOX, and ensure that essential communication workflows are not interrupted during high-stress situations.

Ultimately, MAPI serves as a vital enabler of resilient communication ecosystems that underpin effective business continuity planning. Its ability to automate incident response workflows, support hybrid infrastructures, maintain secure communication, and integrate with broader continuity frameworks ensures that organizations are well-prepared to face unforeseen challenges while safeguarding their operations, employees, and customers.

MAPI Skillsets: What IT Teams Need to Know

As organizations continue to rely on robust messaging infrastructures to support communication, collaboration, and workflow automation, MAPI, or Messaging Application Programming Interface, remains a foundational technology for IT teams working with Microsoft Exchange environments. While MAPI is often perceived as a behind-the-scenes enabler for applications such as Microsoft Outlook, its influence extends deeply into enterprise workflows, custom integrations, and business process automation. For IT professionals, mastering MAPI-related skillsets is critical to maintaining a secure, efficient, and scalable messaging ecosystem. Understanding MAPI architecture, troubleshooting methodologies, security considerations, and development capabilities are all essential areas of expertise for modern IT teams.

The first skill IT teams must acquire is a strong understanding of MAPI's architecture and its role within the broader Exchange ecosystem. MAPI functions as the communication layer that enables applications to interact directly with Exchange servers for accessing mailboxes, calendars, contacts, and tasks. IT teams must be familiar with MAPI over HTTP, the modern transport protocol that replaces legacy RPC over HTTP. MAPI over HTTP offers improved reliability, faster reconnections, and better user experience across hybrid and cloud-based environments. IT professionals should understand how MAPI client requests are routed to Exchange Client Access Services, how session management is handled, and how MAPI integrates with load balancers, firewalls, and authentication services.

Proficiency in configuring and managing Exchange servers is another key skill set related to MAPI. IT teams must know how to properly configure virtual directories, authentication settings, SSL/TLS encryption, and service endpoints to support secure and stable MAPI communication. Knowledge of Exchange administrative tools, such as the Exchange Admin Center and Exchange Management Shell, is essential for tasks like troubleshooting connectivity issues, managing mailbox databases, and configuring high-availability solutions like Database Availability Groups (DAGs). A thorough understanding of Exchange server performance tuning is also important, as MAPI performance is closely tied to the health and efficiency of Exchange infrastructure.

Troubleshooting MAPI-related issues is a core competency for IT teams. Common MAPI challenges include client connection failures, session timeouts, slow performance, and synchronization errors in Outlook. IT professionals must be skilled in interpreting MAPI diagnostic logs, Exchange protocol logs, and client-side error codes. They should know how to use tools like Microsoft Remote Connectivity Analyzer to test MAPI over HTTP connectivity and identify potential issues related to DNS configuration, SSL certificate mismatches, or authentication failures. Additionally, familiarity with Outlook logging features and network tracing tools can assist IT teams in diagnosing issues that impact end-user productivity.

A critical area of expertise is MAPI security. IT teams must implement and enforce secure communication practices, including SSL/TLS encryption for MAPI sessions, integration with Active Directory for authentication, and the use of multi-factor authentication (MFA) for user accounts accessing MAPI services. IT professionals should also be able to configure Exchange to work with security enhancements such as S/MIME, enabling end-to-end encryption and digital signatures for sensitive emails. Understanding how to apply and manage sensitivity labels, data loss prevention (DLP) policies, and transport rules within Exchange ensures that MAPI-enabled communications comply with internal security policies and regulatory requirements.

For IT teams involved in custom development or integration projects, MAPI programming knowledge is another vital skill. MAPI exposes a wide range of functions and interfaces that allow developers to build custom applications capable of automating messaging workflows, manipulating mailbox items, or integrating with third-party business systems. IT professionals should be familiar with C++ and C# for building MAPI-based applications and know how to navigate the complexities of MAPI's COM-based architecture. Key development skills include working with message stores, folders, messages, attachments, and address books programmatically. Additionally, IT teams should understand how to implement proper error handling, session management, and object disposal to avoid memory leaks and ensure scalable application performance.

In hybrid and cloud-first environments, IT professionals must also understand how MAPI integrates with Microsoft 365 and Exchange Online. Skills related to Azure Active Directory, OAuth 2.0 authentication, and Microsoft Graph API are essential for teams supporting organizations with cloud-based Exchange infrastructures. IT teams should know how to configure hybrid Exchange deployments, synchronize identities between on-premises Active Directory and Azure AD, and ensure seamless connectivity between Outlook clients and both on-premises and cloud-hosted mailboxes via MAPI.

Automation is an increasingly important aspect of modern IT operations, and IT teams should be capable of automating common MAPI-related administrative tasks. Familiarity with scripting languages such as PowerShell enables IT professionals to automate mailbox provisioning, apply mailbox permissions, generate audit reports, and enforce retention policies across MAPI-enabled environments. Automation reduces manual workload, improves consistency, and enhances the scalability of Exchange and MAPI management processes.

Another essential skill is monitoring and reporting. IT teams should implement monitoring solutions that provide visibility into MAPI session health, resource utilization, and user experience. Integrating MAPI logs and performance metrics with security information and event management (SIEM) platforms allows IT professionals to proactively detect anomalies, troubleshoot issues, and generate actionable insights. Developing custom dashboards in tools like Microsoft System Center Operations Manager (SCOM) or Power BI enables IT teams to track key indicators such as session establishment times, server load distribution, and MAPI-related error trends.

Soft skills such as documentation and communication are equally important. IT teams must document MAPI configuration baselines, troubleshooting procedures, and security policies to ensure knowledge transfer and support continuity. Effective communication skills help IT professionals explain technical concepts to non-technical stakeholders, coordinate with development teams on integration projects, and provide training to end users on how to resolve basic MAPI-related issues in Outlook.

Finally, continuous learning is crucial for IT teams supporting MAPI environments. As Microsoft evolves its Exchange platform and related technologies, IT professionals must stay current with new features, updates, and best practices. Participating in training programs, certifications such as Microsoft Certified: Messaging Administrator Associate, and attending industry conferences or webinars ensures that IT teams remain well-equipped to manage and optimize MAPI-enabled infrastructures.

In summary, IT teams supporting MAPI environments require a diverse skill set that spans Exchange server management, troubleshooting expertise, security enforcement, custom application development, automation, and monitoring. By mastering these areas, IT professionals can ensure that MAPI-based communication workflows operate efficiently, securely, and in alignment with the organization's broader business objectives. In a world where seamless communication is essential to business success, the ability to effectively manage and optimize MAPI-enabled systems is a critical competency for modern IT teams.

The Competitive Advantage of MAPI Integration

In an increasingly connected and technology-driven business landscape, achieving a competitive advantage often depends on an organization's ability to optimize communication, streamline operations, and integrate technology seamlessly into core business processes. MAPI, or Messaging Application Programming Interface, has traditionally been recognized for enabling applications such as Microsoft Outlook to interact with Microsoft Exchange servers. However, when fully leveraged, MAPI integration offers organizations more than just messaging functionality—it serves as a catalyst for operational efficiency, agility, and strategic differentiation. Businesses that embed MAPI deeply into their workflows and systems can unlock tangible advantages over competitors who rely on fragmented or manual communication processes.

One of the most significant competitive advantages provided by MAPI integration is operational efficiency. MAPI allows organizations to automate and streamline messaging workflows that are critical to business operations. Whether it is automatically generating and sending order confirmations, routing customer service requests to the appropriate department, or updating shared calendars with project milestones, MAPI ensures that communication tasks occur in real time with minimal human intervention. This automation reduces manual workload, lowers the risk of errors, and accelerates business processes.

For example, a company that uses MAPI to automate client onboarding emails and task assignments can deliver a faster, more seamless experience compared to competitors still relying on manual coordination.

Speed is another core competitive advantage facilitated by MAPI. In today's fast-paced business environment, the ability to respond quickly to customer inquiries, internal escalations, or supply chain disruptions can determine whether an organization wins or loses critical opportunities. MAPI supports rapid and reliable communication by integrating directly with Exchange environments, enabling the automatic dissemination of information across teams and systems. Sales organizations can benefit from automated follow-up emails and meeting invitations generated through MAPI workflows, helping sales representatives engage prospects more quickly and effectively than competitors operating with slower or disjointed processes.

MAPI also provides a competitive edge by enhancing data consistency and integration across business platforms. When communication systems operate in silos, data inconsistencies and communication breakdowns are common. MAPI acts as a bridge between email systems and critical business applications, such as ERP, CRM, and project management tools. This integration ensures that information captured in email communications is synchronized with other systems, improving data accuracy and enabling a single source of truth across the organization. For example, sales-related emails containing order details, client requirements, or project updates can be automatically logged into the CRM system using MAPI-based applications, reducing administrative overhead and ensuring that customer records are always up to date.

The ability to deliver a superior customer experience is another significant differentiator that MAPI integration offers. Customers expect timely, accurate, and personalized communication from businesses. MAPI enables organizations to automate customer engagement touchpoints, such as personalized email confirmations, appointment reminders, and follow-up communications. By connecting customer data from CRM systems to automated messaging workflows via MAPI, businesses can deliver highly tailored communications that demonstrate attention to detail and responsiveness. A competitor without such automated personalization capabilities may struggle to build the same level of customer loyalty and satisfaction.

MAPI also enhances collaboration and transparency within organizations, contributing to better decision-making and project execution. Integrated MAPI workflows ensure that key stakeholders receive real-time updates, meeting requests, and project-related notifications automatically, reducing delays and improving team coordination. For example, in a construction project, MAPI can be used to automate calendar invites for milestone reviews, generate email alerts when project risks are identified, and share updated documentation directly from the project management system to the appropriate teams. By embedding communication deeply into project workflows, organizations can deliver projects on time and on budget, giving them an advantage over competitors facing internal miscommunication and delays.

Security and compliance are other areas where MAPI integration provides a competitive edge, particularly in regulated industries such as healthcare, finance, and legal services. MAPI supports secure messaging by enabling end-to-end encryption, integration with S/MIME, and the application of sensitivity labels through Microsoft Exchange. Automated workflows built on MAPI can enforce organizational security policies by automatically classifying and archiving sensitive communications, ensuring compliance with regulations such as GDPR, HIPAA, and SOX. By demonstrating strong security and compliance practices, organizations can build trust with customers, partners, and regulators, positioning themselves as reliable and responsible market leaders.

For organizations operating globally, MAPI integration supports localization and scalability of communication strategies. MAPI workflows can automatically generate multilingual communications, adjust appointment times based on time zones, and route messages to region-specific teams or systems. This adaptability allows businesses to deliver a consistent and culturally relevant experience to customers and partners worldwide. Competitors lacking such capabilities may face challenges in maintaining global consistency and responsiveness, especially when managing cross-border operations.

Another area where MAPI integration enhances competitiveness is in supporting business continuity and resilience. By automating incident notifications, scheduling crisis response meetings, and ensuring that essential messaging workflows remain operational during disruptions, MAPI helps businesses respond to crises more effectively. Organizations with resilient MAPI-based communication systems can minimize downtime, maintain customer communication, and coordinate recovery efforts faster than competitors unprepared for unexpected events.

MAPI's role in enabling advanced analytics and business intelligence further strengthens its competitive value. By extracting and integrating messaging data with analytics platforms, businesses can gain insights into communication patterns, customer engagement trends, and internal workflow performance. These insights empower leaders to make data-driven decisions, refine communication strategies, and optimize resource allocation. For instance, analyzing how quickly customer inquiries are addressed or how internal teams collaborate on projects can reveal opportunities for process improvement that competitors may overlook.

The flexibility of MAPI also allows organizations to build custom solutions tailored to their unique business needs. Whether creating custom Outlook add-ins, automating document approval workflows, or integrating with industry-specific applications, MAPI offers the versatility to deliver bespoke functionality that aligns with business goals. Organizations that invest in custom MAPI solutions can differentiate themselves with proprietary workflows, enhanced user experiences, and faster time to market for new initiatives. Competitors reliant on generic or out-of-the-box communication tools may struggle to achieve the same level of operational alignment and innovation.

Ultimately, MAPI integration supports the strategic agility required to thrive in rapidly evolving markets. As businesses adopt hybrid work models, expand into new markets, or implement digital transformation initiatives, MAPI provides a scalable and adaptable framework for communication automation and integration. Organizations that leverage MAPI effectively can respond to changing market demands, regulatory requirements, and technological advancements faster and more efficiently than less agile competitors.

By embedding MAPI into the fabric of enterprise communication and workflow systems, businesses unlock a competitive advantage rooted in operational efficiency, customer satisfaction, security, and innovation. In a landscape where speed, reliability, and seamless integration are crucial to success, MAPI provides the tools to empower organizations to outpace competitors, deliver exceptional value to customers, and continuously improve business performance.

The Future of MAPI and Business Communication Systems

The future of MAPI, or Messaging Application Programming Interface, is intrinsically linked to the ongoing evolution of business communication systems as organizations continue to adapt to digital transformation, remote work, and cloud-first strategies. MAPI has historically been a crucial component in enabling Microsoft Outlook to interact with Microsoft Exchange servers, powering email, calendaring, and task management functions. However, as businesses move toward more integrated, flexible, and intelligent communication ecosystems, MAPI is poised to play a renewed and evolving role in supporting next-generation workflows and collaboration models.

One of the key trends shaping the future of MAPI is the growing demand for seamless integration between communication tools and broader enterprise ecosystems. As organizations increasingly adopt hybrid and multi-cloud environments, MAPI's role will expand to bridge messaging systems with cloud-native applications, third-party platforms, and business-critical workflows. MAPI will continue to evolve in parallel with Microsoft Exchange, ensuring it remains a viable integration point for both on-premises and cloud-hosted Exchange environments. As businesses transition to Microsoft 365 and hybrid infrastructures, MAPI over HTTP will remain the standard protocol, supporting secure and efficient messaging traffic across distributed environments.

The convergence of artificial intelligence and machine learning with business communication platforms will also influence the future of

MAPI. AI-driven features such as predictive email composition, intelligent scheduling, and automated document classification will become more deeply embedded within communication workflows. MAPI's programmatic capabilities will be leveraged by developers to integrate AI-powered bots and virtual assistants directly into Outlook and Exchange environments. For example, future MAPI workflows could enable AI agents to automatically prioritize incoming messages, suggest responses based on historical communication patterns, or coordinate meeting scheduling without human intervention. These advancements will transform MAPI from a purely transactional protocol into a critical enabler of intelligent, automated communication processes.

As the hybrid workplace model becomes permanent for many organizations, MAPI's ability to support consistent and secure communication across remote and in-office teams will remain vital. Businesses will continue to rely on MAPI to ensure that users can access their mailboxes, shared calendars, and collaborative task lists regardless of location. The emphasis on employee productivity and seamless user experiences will drive enhancements in MAPI-enabled client applications, making them more responsive, resilient, and adaptable to varying network conditions. Features such as faster session recovery, optimized caching, and enhanced offline capabilities will continue to improve the end-user experience in remote work scenarios.

MAPI will also play a pivotal role in the expansion of unified communications (UC) platforms. As organizations seek to consolidate email, chat, voice, video conferencing, and document sharing into integrated environments, MAPI will provide the necessary backend integration to ensure email and calendar data are synchronized with UC tools. For example, a UC platform may leverage MAPI to automatically pull calendar data from Exchange and display availability information within a real-time collaboration interface. Similarly, MAPI-based workflows will enable automated logging of email communications into UC platforms, ensuring that all relevant conversation histories and action items are accessible to teams collaborating within a single platform.

Another emerging factor influencing the future of MAPI is the heightened focus on security and compliance. As cyber threats grow more sophisticated and regulatory requirements become stricter, MAPI will continue to evolve to support advanced security measures. Future MAPI deployments will integrate more closely with Zero Trust architectures, enforcing stricter authentication and authorization protocols, such as conditional access policies and continuous risk assessments. Additionally, MAPI workflows will increasingly incorporate automated data protection mechanisms, such as encryption enforcement, information rights management, and adaptive sensitivity labeling based on message content. These features will help organizations meet compliance requirements while safeguarding sensitive business communications from internal and external threats.

The role of MAPI in supporting real-time business insights will also become more pronounced. MAPI's ability to interface with Exchange metadata and messaging content makes it an invaluable source of operational data. As more organizations invest in analytics platforms and business intelligence tools, MAPI will serve as a critical data conduit, feeding structured and unstructured communication data into advanced analytics engines. Businesses will leverage this data to gain deeper insights into customer engagement patterns, employee productivity trends, and workflow bottlenecks. In future deployments, MAPI-enabled applications may integrate directly with AI-driven analytics tools, providing organizations with real-time dashboards and predictive models to optimize communication and collaboration strategies.

The continued rise of low-code and no-code development platforms will also impact how MAPI is utilized. As business users and citizen developers increasingly seek to automate workflows without deep programming expertise, MAPI will be abstracted and made accessible through simplified integration frameworks. Organizations will use low-code platforms to build custom applications and automation routines that connect MAPI-powered messaging systems with other enterprise tools, such as CRM solutions, HR platforms, and document management systems. This democratization of integration capabilities will enable faster innovation and allow business units to address specific communication needs without waiting for IT-led development cycles.

Interoperability will be another key theme in the future of MAPI. With many organizations operating diverse technology ecosystems, MAPI will increasingly need to coexist and integrate with other industry-standard protocols and APIs. For example, businesses using Google Workspace, Slack, or Salesforce alongside Microsoft Exchange will require MAPI-based workflows to synchronize communication data and maintain consistency across platforms. To support this demand, MAPI will continue to integrate with API gateways, middleware platforms, and microservices architectures that facilitate cross-platform data exchange and orchestration.

Sustainability and energy efficiency will also influence future MAPI deployments. As organizations prioritize green IT initiatives, reducing the energy consumption and environmental impact of IT infrastructure will become a key consideration. Optimizing MAPI communication patterns, minimizing server resource usage, and leveraging cloud-native optimizations will help organizations align their messaging environments with sustainability goals. Cloud providers will also play a role by offering MAPI-compatible services that operate on energy-efficient infrastructure.

In summary, the future of MAPI will be shaped by the broader evolution of business communication systems toward intelligence, automation, and integration. As organizations pursue digital transformation, hybrid work enablement, and operational resilience, MAPI will remain a foundational technology that enables seamless communication workflows across diverse environments. Whether supporting AI-driven automation, enhancing security and compliance, or integrating with next-generation collaboration platforms, MAPI will continue to evolve as a vital component of enterprise communication ecosystems, empowering businesses to thrive in an increasingly dynamic and interconnected world.